Quod scriptura, non iubet vetat

The Latin translates, "What is not commanded in scripture, is forbidden:'

On the Cover: Baptists rejoice to hold in common with other evangelicals the main principles of the orthodox Christian faith. However, there are points of difference and these differences are significant. In fact, because these differences arise out of God's revealed will, they are of vital importance. Hence, the barriers of separation between Baptists and others can hardly be considered a trifling matter. To suppose that Baptists are kept apart solely by their views on Baptism or the Lord's Supper is a regrettable misunderstanding. Baptists hold views which distinguish them from Catholics, Congregationalists, Episcopalians, Lutherans, Methodists, Pentecostals, and Presbyterians, and the differences are so great as not only to justify, but to demand, the separate denominational existence of Baptists. Some people think Baptists ought not teach and emphasize their differences but as E.J. Forrester stated in 1893, "Any denomination that has views which justify its separate existence, is bound to promulgate those views. If those views are of sufficient importance to justify a separate existence, they are important enough to create a duty for their promulgation ... the very same reasons which justify the separate existence of any denomination make it the duty of that denomination to teach the distinctive doctrines upon which its separate existence rests." If Baptists have a right to a separate denominational life, it is their duty to propagate their distinctive principles, without which their separate life cannot be justified or maintained.

Many among today's professing Baptists have an agenda to revise the Baptist distinctives and redefine what it means to be a Baptist. Others don't understand why it even matters. The books being reproduced in the *Baptist Distinctives Series* are republished in order that Baptists from the past may state, explain and defend the primary Baptist distinctives as they understood them. It is hoped that this Series will provide a more thorough historical perspective on what it means to be distinctively Baptist.

The Lord Jesus Christ asked, *"And why call ye me, Lord, Lord, and do not the things which I say?"* (Luke 6:46). The immediate context surrounding this question explains what it means to be a true disciple of Christ. Addressing the same issue, Christ's question is meant to show that a confession of discipleship to the Lord Jesus Christ is inconsistent and untrue if it is not accompanied with a corresponding submission to His authoritative commands. Christ's question teaches us that a true recognition of His authority as Lord inevitably includes a submission to the authority of His Word. Hence, with this question Christ has made it forever impossible to separate His authority as King from the authority of His Word. These two principles—the authority of Christ as King and the authority of His Word—are the two most fundamental Baptist distinctives. The first gives rise to the second and out of these two all the other Baptist distinctives emanate. As F.M. Iams wrote in 1894, "Loyalty to Christ as King, manifesting itself in a constant and unswerving obedience to His will as revealed in His written Word, is the real source of all the Baptist distinctives:' In the search for the *primary* Baptist distinctive many have settled on the Lordship of Christ as the most basic distinctive. Strangely, in doing this, some have attempted to separate Christ's Lordship from the authority of Scripture, as if you could embrace Christ's authority without submitting to what He commanded. However, while Christ's Lordship and Kingly authority can be isolated and considered essentially for discussion's sake, we see from Christ's own words in Luke 6:46 that His Lordship is really inseparable from His Word and, with regard to real Christian discipleship, there can be no practical submission to the one without a practical submission to the other.

In the symbol above the Kingly Crown and the Open Bible represent the inseparable truths of Christ's Kingly and Biblical authority. The Crown and Bible graphics are supplemented by three Bible verses (Ecclesiastes 8:4, Matthew 28:18-20, and Luke 6:46) that reiterate and reinforce the inextricable connection between the authority of Christ as King and the authority of His Word. The truths symbolized by these components are further emphasized by the Latin quotation - *quod scriptura, non iubet vetat*— *i.e.,* "What is not commanded in scripture, is forbidden:' This Latin quote has been considered historically as a summary statement of the regulative principle of Scripture. Together these various symbolic components converge to exhibit the two most foundational Baptist Distinctives out of which all the other Baptist Distinctives arise. Consequently, we have chosen this composite symbol as a logo to represent the primary truths set forth in the *Baptist Distinctives Series.*

Ecclesia:
The Church

B. H. CARROLL
(1843-1914)

Ecclesia:
THE CHURCH

Bible Class Lecture
February, 1903

Complete and Unabridged

BY

B. H. Carroll

DEAN THEOLOGICAL DEPARTMENT
BAYLOR UNIVERSITY

With a Biographical Sketch of the Author by John Franklin Jones

---

LOUISVILLE, KENTUCKY
1903

he Baptist Standard Bearer, Inc.
NUMBER ONE IRON OAKS DRIVE • PARIS, ARKANSAS 72855

Thou hast given a *standard* to them that fear thee;
that it may be displayed because of the truth.
-- *Psalm 60:4*

Reprinted 2006

by

THE BAPTIST STANDARD BEARER, INC.
No. 1 Iron Oaks Drive
Paris, Arkansas 72855
(479) 963-3831

THE WALDENSIAN EMBLEM
lux lucet in tenebris
"The Light Shineth in the Darkness"

ISBN# 1579783252

TABLE OF CONTENTS

ECCLESIA—THE CHURCH

---※---

	Page
ECCLESIA—THE CHURCH: LECTURE 1 *The Etymology of the Greek Word Ecclesia*	13
APPENDIX NO. 1 ***Usage of the Greek word Ecclesia***	33
Its Usage in the Classical Greek	35
Its Usage in the Septuagint	39
Its Usage in the Apocrypha	43
Its Usage in the New Testament	47
ECCLESIA—THE CHURCH: LECTURE 2 *Questions About the Etymology and Usage of the Greek Word Ecclesia*	53
I. "As in the Septuagint *ecclesia* translates the Hebrew word *gahal,* does it not mean, All Israel, whether assembled or unassembled?"	55
II. "Do not some of these *Septuagint* passages justify the meaning of *unassembled?*"	56

TABLE OF CONTENTS, CONT.

III.
"As Christ was establishing a new institution, widely different from the Greek state ecclesia, was not *ecclesia* in the New Testament used in a new, special and sacred sense?" 57

IV.
"But when Paul says, I persecuted the *church*, surely that can only mean that he persecuted the disciples?" 59

V.
"But if the church means *assembly* does not that require it to be always in session?" 59

VI.
"But if the *earthly ecclesia* exists now, though many of its members forsake the assembling of themselves together, and if it continually receives new members, why may we not say the *general assembly* exists now, though all be not actually assembled, nor all its members yet born?" 59

VII.
"You ask for a particular explanation of several Scriptures which seem difficult to harmonize with the contentions of the first lecture, all of which in turn will now receive attention." 62

VIII.
"The next class of Scriptures which you wish explained is represented by Ephesians 1:22-23; Colossians 1:18; 1 Peter 2:5; Hebrews 3:6; John 10:16." 66

IX.
"There remain for consideration only two other Scriptures and then all your questions are answered, Ephesians 5:25-27; Hebrews 12:18-24. And these will receive particular attention because they were cited in the first lecture." 68

APPENDIX NO. 2
Additional Sermons About Baptist Distinctives by B.H. Carroll 75

BAPTISM IN WATER 79

A DISCUSSION OF THE LORD'S SUPPER 107

DISTINCTIVE BAPTIST PRINCIPLES 143

APPENDIX NO. 3
Why Should We Try to Win Protestants to Baptist Views
DR. JOHN A. BRODUS 165

A BIOGRAPHICAL SKETCH OF B.H. CARROLL (1843-1914)
BY JOHN FRANKLIN JONES 169

ECCLESIA — THE CHURCH

LECTURE 1.

The Etymology of the Greek Word Ecclesia

Matthew 16:18-19

IN regular course the class has arrived at the first New Testament use of the Greek word *ecclesia,* here rendered "church."

This passage, Matt. 16:18, 19, has been for many centuries a battle-ground of theological controversies. Though millions of the disputants have passed away, the questions which arrayed them against each other still survive to align their successors in hostile array.

The most important of these divisive questions are:

    1. What is the church?

    2. Who established it and when?

    3. What the foundation?

    4. What the "gates of hell?"

    5. What the "keys?"

    6. What the "binding and loosing?"

In replying to these questions it should constantly be borne in mind, that all the intelligence, piety, sincerity and scholarship of the world are not monopolized by any one age, nor by any one denomination. Still less does infallibility of interpretation belong to any one party of conflicting views within a single denomination. And yet still less may any one man assume that wisdom on this subject will die with him. It becomes a single teacher, therefore, to be modest, and while he may not from the nature of the case avoid dogmatism, let him at least shun *offensive* dogmatism and be duly considerate of the feelings of others.

Of one thing you may be assured, that these questions cannot be satisfactorily answered by any human *ipse dixit.* Nor is there the slightest hope of solution in appeals to human creeds and histories. These are as variant and conflicting as their composers and all are without a shred of authority.

Let it be enough for us to seek a solution satisfactory to our own mind in the study for ourselves of the Bible alone.

You will understand, therefore, that the conclusions herein set forth, though reached by careful, prayerful and honest study of the one book alone, are worth no more than their intrinsic merit may warrant, and that having already given you a list of all the New Testament uses of the word, you are left entirely free to test every conclusion for yourselves, by the given usage, and then to accept, modify or reject it, as your own judgment and conscience may direct.

In this lecture there will be time for answer to the first question only:

WHAT IS THE CHURCH?

From the given list of passages, taken from the Englishman's Greek Concordance, and which you may verify by reference to the Bible, it appears that the word *Ecclesia,* usually rendered "church" in our version, occurs 117 times in the Greek New Testament (omitting Acts 2:47 as not in the best texts).

Our Lord and the New Testament writers neither coined this word nor employed it in any unusual sense. Before their time

Ecclesia — The Church

it was in common use, of well-understood signification, and subject like any other word to varied employment, according to the established laws of language.

That is, it might be used abstractly, or generically, or particularly, or prospectively, without losing its essential meaning.

To simplify and shorten the work before us, we need not leave the New Testament to find examples of its classic or Septuagint use. Fair examples of both are in the list of New Testament passages given you.

What, then, etymologically, is the meaning of this word?

Its primary meaning is: An organized assembly, whose members have been properly called out from private homes or business to attend to public affairs. This definition necessarily implies prescribed conditions of membership.

This meaning, substantially, applies alike to the *ecclesia* of a self-governing Greek state (Acts 19:39), the Old Testament *ecclesia,* or convocation of National Israel (Acts 7:38), and to the New Testament *ecclesia.*

When, in this lesson, our Lord says: "On this rock I will build my *ecclesia,*" while the "my" distinguished his *ecclesia* from the Greek state *ecclesia* and the Old Testament *ecclesia,* the word itself naturally retains its ordinary meaning.

Indeed, even when by accommodation it is applied to an irregular gathering (Acts 19:32, 41) the essential idea of *assembly* remains.

Of the 117 instances of use in the New Testament certainly all but five (Acts 7:38; 19:32, 39, 42; Heb. 2:12) refer to Christ's *ecclesia*. And since Hebrews 2:12, though a quotation from the Old Testament, is prophetic, finding fulfillment in New Testament times, we need not regard it as an exception. These 113 uses of the word, including Hebrews 2:12, refer either to the *particular assembly* of Jesus Christ on earth, or to his *general assembly* in glory.

Commonly, that is in nearly all the uses, it means, The particular assembly of Christ's baptized disciples on earth, as "The church of God which is at Corinth."

To this class necessarily belong all abstract or generic uses of the word, for whenever the abstract or generic finds concrete expression, or takes operative shape, it is always a particular assembly.

This follows from the laws of language governing the use of words.

For example, if an English statesman, referring to the right of each individual citizen to be tried by his peers, should say: "On this rock England will build her jury and all the power of tyrants shall not prevail against it," he uses the term jury in an *abstract* sense, *i.e.*, in the sense of an *institution*. But when this institution *finds* concrete expression, or becomes operative, it is always a particular jury of twelve men, and never in an aggregation of all juries into one big jury.

Or if a law writer should say: "In trials of fact, by oral testimony, the court shall be the judge of the law, and the jury shall be the judge of the facts," and if he should add: "In giving evidence, the witness shall tell what he knows to the jury, and not to the court," he evidently uses the terms "court," "jury" and "witness," in a generic sense. But in the application the *generic* always becomes particular—*i.e.*, a particular judge, a particular jury, or a particular witness, and never an aggregate of all judges into one big judge, nor of all juries into one big jury, nor of all witnesses into one big witness. Hence we say that the laws of language require that all abstract and generic uses of the word *ecclesia* should be classified with the particular assembly and not with the general assembly.

As examples of the abstract use of *ecclesia* that is in the sense of an *institution,* we cite Matt. 16:18; Eph. 3:10, 21.

Ecclesia — THE CHURCH

Matt. 18:17 is an example of generic use. That is, it designates the *kind* (genus) of tribunal to which difficulties must be referred without restriction of application to any one particular church by name. I mean that while its application must always be to a particular church, yet it is not restricted to just one, as the church at Jerusalem, but is equally applicable to every other particular church.

As when Paul says: "The husband is the head of the wife," the terms "husband" and "wife" are not to be restricted in application to John Jones and his wife, but apply equally to every other specific husband and wife.

But while nearly all of the 113 instances of the use of *ecclesia* belong to the particular class, there are some instances, as Heb. 12:23, and Eph. 5:25-27, where the reference seems to be to the general assembly of Christ. But in every such case the *ecclesia* is *prospective,* not actual. That is to say, there is *not* now but there *will be* a general assembly of Christ's people. That general assembly will be composed of all the redeemed of all time.

Here are three indisputable and very significant facts concerning Christ's General Assembly:

(1) Many of its members, properly called out, are now in heaven.

(2) Many others of them, also called out, are here on earth.

(3) Indefinite millions of them, probably the great majority, yet to be called, are neither on earth nor in heaven, because they are yet unborn, and therefore non-existent.

It follows that if one part of the membership is now in heaven, another part on earth, another part not yet born, *there is as yet no assembly,* except in prospect.

And if a part, probably the majority, are as yet non-existent, how can one say the General Assembly *exists now*?

We may, however, properly speak of the General Assembly now, because, though part of it is yet non-existent, and though there has not yet been a gathering together of the other two parts yet, the mind may *conceive* of that gathering as an accomplished fact.

In God's purposes and plans, the General Assembly exists now, and also in our conceptions of anticipations, but certainly not as a fact. The details of God's purpose are now being worked out, and the process will continue until all the elect have been called, justified, glorified and *assembled*.

Commenting on our lesson, Dr. Broadus says:

> "In the New Testament the *spiritual* Israel, never actually assembled, is sometimes conceived of as an ideal congregation or assembly, and this is denoted by the word *ecclesia*."

Here Dr. B. does not contrast "spiritual Israel" with a particular church of Christ, but with national or carnal Israel.

The object of the gospel, committed to the particular assembly in time, is to call out or summon those who shall compose the General Assembly in eternity.

When the calling out is ended and all the called are glorified, then the present concept of a General Assembly will be a fact. Then and only then *actually,* will all the redeemed be an *ecclesia*. Moreover, this *ecclesia in glory* will be the real body, temple, flock or bride of our Lord.

But the only *existing* representation or type of the *ecclesia in glory* (*i.e.,* the General Assembly) is the particular assembly on earth.

And because each and every particular assembly is the representation, or type, of the General Assembly, to each and every one of them is applied all the broad figures which pertain to the General Assembly. That is, such figures as "the house of God," "the temple of the Lord," "the body," or "flock" or "bride of Christ." The New Testament applies these figures, just as freely and frequently, to the particular assembly as to the General Assembly. That is, to any one particular assembly, by itself alone, but never to all the particular assemblies *collectively.*

There is no unity, no organization, nor gathering together and, hence, no *ecclesia* or assembly of particular congregations collectively. So also the term *ecclesia* cannot be rationally applied to all denominations collectively, nor to all living professors of religion, nor to all living believers collectively. In no sense are any such unassembled aggregates an *ecclesia.* None of them constitutes the flock, bride, temple, body or house of God, either as a type of time or a reality of eternity. These terms belong exclusively either to the particular assembly now or the General Assembly hereafter.

A man once said to me, How dare you apply such broad terms as "The house of God," "The body of Christ," "The temple of the Lord," to your little fragment of a denomination? My reply was, I do not apply them to any denomination, nor to any aggregate of the particular congregations of any or of all denominations, but the Scriptures do apply every one of them to a particular New Testament congregation of Christ's disciples.

Hear the Word of God:

In the letter to the Ephesians, Paul says: "In whom each several building, fitly framed together, groweth into a holy temple in the Lord; in whom ye also are builded together for a habitation of God in the Spirit." (Eph. 2:21, 22, R.V.)

Here are two distinct affirmations:

First— Each several building or particular assembly groweth into a holy temple of the Lord. That is, by itself it is a temple of the Lord.

Second— What is true of each is true of the church at Ephesus, "In whom ye also are builded together for a habitation of God through the Spirit."

Just before this he had written of the church as an *institution,* or abstractly, in which Jew and Gentile are made into one. But the abstract becomes concrete in each several building.

To the elders of this same particular church at Ephesus he said: "Take heed to yourselves, and to *all the flock,* in which the Holy Spirit hath made you bishops, to *feed the church of the Lord* which he purchased with his own blood." —Acts 20:28.

This flock, this church of the Lord, purchased by his own blood, is a particular assembly.

Again to the particular church at Corinth Paul wrote: "Ye are God's building—ye are *a temple* of God and the Spirit dwelleth in you—now ye are the *body* of Christ, and severally members thereof." (1 Cor. 3:7, 16; 12:27.)

When concerning the body of Christ he says: "And whether one member suffereth all the members suffer with it," he is certainly not speaking of the *Ecclesia in Glory,* all of whose members will be *past* sufferings when constituting an e*cclesia.*

Again concerning the particular church at Ephesus, he writes to Timothy whom he had left in that city: "These things write I unto thee, hoping to come unto thee shortly; but if I tarry long, that thou mayest know, how men ought to behave themselves in the house of God, which is the church of the living God, the pillar and ground of the truth." He is certainly not writing of behavior in the general assembly in glory. The things he had written touching behavior were, when and how the men should pray, how the women should dress and work, and the qualifications of bishops and deacons. Even that remarkable passage, so often and so confidently quoted as referring exclusively to some supposed now existing "universal, invisible, spiritual church," namely: Eph. 1:22, 23, "And gave him to be head over all things to the church, which is his body, the fullness of him that filleth all in all"—even this very body, "filled unto all the fullness of God," *is presently applied, in his prayer, to the particular congregation* (Eph. 3:19).

But it may be asked how could Paul pray that a particular congregation might be filled unto all the fullness of God? The reply is obvious. Each particular assembly is an habitation of God through the Spirit. The Spirit occupies each several building. Into each he enters not with partial power, but in all the fullness of Omnipotent power.

But though the fullness is there, the church is so dim-eyed, so weak in faith—so feeble in graces—it does not realize and lay hold of and appropriate this fullness of God. Hence the prayer that the eyes of their understanding might be open to see the fullness, their faith increased to grasp and appropriate it, their graces enlarged to corresponding strength to stand and work in that fullness. So fulfilled they realize in *experience* the fact that the Holy Spirit in all the fullness of God had already entered this particular body of Christ, and was only waiting to be recognized. It is like the expression, "Being justified by faith, let us have peace with God," etc., Rom. 5:1. That is, we are entitled to it, let us take it.

In a great revival of religion we see Paul's prayer fulfilled in the particular body of Christ. Gradually the church warms up to a realization of the fullness of God dwelling in them through the Spirit. Their spiritual apprehension becomes eagle-eyed. The grasp of their faith becomes the grip of a giant. Presently they say, we "can do all things." No barrier is now insurmountable. And as more and more they comprehend the height and depth and width and length of the love of God, they glow like a spiritual furnace. Thus it is proven that all these broad terms appertaining to the future general assembly are equally applied to the present particular assembly, and that, too, because it is the only existing representation of the prospective general assembly.

This leads to another conclusion:

All teaching in the direction that there now exists a general assembly which is invisible, without ordinances, and which is entered by faith alone, will likely tend to discredit the particular assembly, which does now really exist and which is the pillar and ground of the truth.

More than once when I have inquired of a man, "are you a member of the church?" the reply has been, "I am a member of the invisible, universal, spiritual church."

To make faith the exclusive term of admission into the general assembly is more than questionable and naturally generates such replies.

The general assembly, by all accounts includes all the saved. But infants, dying in infancy, are a part of the saved. Yet never having been subjects of gospel address they are saved without faith. But it may be said that such use of the term faith is only a way of saying "a new heart," and dying infants are not without regeneration. To which we may rejoin that regeneration alone is not sufficient to qualify for membership in the general assembly. All the regenerates we know have spots and wrinkles, while the Bride, the general assembly, is without spot or wrinkle, or any such thing.

Nor does complete sanctification of soul go far enough. There must also be glorification of body. Enoch, Elijah and probably those who rose from the dead after Christ's resurrection are the only ones as yet qualified for membership in the general assembly. And they must wait until all whom God has called and will yet call have arrived with like qualifications, before there can be a general assembly in fact.

As has been intimated, all organized assemblies have prescribed terms or conditions of membership. In the Greek

Ecclesia — The Church

state *Ecclesia* membership was limited to a well-defined body of citizens. Not all residents of the territory could participate in the business of the ecclesia. So with the Old Testament *ecclesia* or national convocation of carnal Israel. One must have the required lineal descent and be circumcised or become a proselyte and be circumcised. Correspondingly the conditions of membership in the church on earth are regeneration and baptism.

But for the church in glory the conditions of membership are justification, regeneration and sanctification of soul and glorification of body.

We submit another conclusion:

Some terms or descriptives commonly applied to the church by writers and speakers are not only extra-Scriptural, that is, purely human and post-apostolic, but may he so used as to become either misleading or positively unscriptural. For example, to put *visible*, referring to the particular assembly alone, over against *spiritual* as referring to the general assembly alone, as if these terms were opposites or incompatible with each other.

The particular assembly or church that now is, is both visible and spiritual.

To confess Christ before men, to let our light shine before men, to be baptized, to *show forth* the Lord's death in the Supper, are both visible and spiritual acts of obedience. And when the General Assembly becomes a reality instead of a prospect, it, too, will be both visible and spiritual.

Speaking of the General Assembly, John says: "I *saw* the holy city, the New Jerusalem, coming down out of heaven from God, made ready as a bride adorned for her husband."

When the King came to the earth in his humiliation he was visible. And when he *appears* in glory every eye shall see him.

A city set upon an earthly hill cannot be hid. And the New Jerusalem on Mt. Zion, the city of the living God, will be the most conspicuous and luminous object the universe ever saw.

The confusion wrought by these human appellatives is manifest in the growth of what is commonly mis-called "the Apostle's creed." In its earliest historic forms it says: "I believe in the holy church." Later forms say: "I believe in the holy catholic, *i.e.,* universal church." Still later: "in the holy catholic and apostolic church." Still gathering increment from other creeds it becomes: "The holy Roman catholic and apostolic church." Then comes "visible vs. invisible," or "visible, temporal, universal vs. invisible, spiritual, universal," and so *ad infinitum*. But the Bible in its simplicity knows nothing of these scholastic refinements of distinction. In that holy book the existing church is a particular congregation of Christ's baptized disciples, and the prospective church is the General Assembly. But mark you; *these are not co-existent.*

One cannot be a member of both at the same time. When the General Assembly comes the particular assembly will have passed away.

To impress more deeply the scripturalness of these reflections, let us consider the subject from another viewpoint:

A house is built for an inhabitant. Unless the tenant is hard pressed, he will not move in until the building is completed. God is never hard pressed.

A long time may be consumed in getting out and gathering together and preparing the material of a house. It is not a house, however, except in purpose, plan or prospect, until it is completed and ready for its occupant.

In this light let us take a look at some Bible houses:

(a) The house that Moses built.

Ecclesia — The Church

This was the Tabernacle of the Wilderness, or tent for God. The 40th chapter of Exodus tells of the completion of this house. When it was finished and all things ready for the occupant it became a house, and then the cloud, that symbol of Divine glory, moved in and filled the tabernacle.

(b) The house that Solomon built.

The 6th, 7th and 8th chapters of 1 Kings tell us about this house. When it was finished and furnished and dedicated, it also being now a house, then the cloud symbol of divine presence and glory, that had inhabited the tabernacle, left the tent as no longer useful and moved into and filled the new house.

(c) The house that Jesus built.

The gospel histories tell us about it. John the Baptist prepared much material for it. Receiving this material from John, and adding much of his own preparation, Jesus built a house. That is, he instituted his *ecclesia* on earth. At his death the veil of Solomon's restored house was rent in twain from top to bottom. Henceforward, it was tenantless, and being useless, soon perished. But though the new house was built, it was empty until our Lord ascended into heaven, and fulfilled his promise to send the Holy Spirit as the indweller of this new habitation. Acts 2 tells us how this house was occupied. The useless temple of Solomon now passes away as the useless tabernacle of Moses passed away for its successor. The only house of God now existing on earth is the particular *ecclesia of* our Lord. But it in turn must have a successor in the General Assembly, or,

(d) The house Jesus will build.

The tabernacle, the temple and the church on earth are all forecasts of the coming church in glory. The work of gathering and preparing material for the General Assembly has been in progress for six thousand years. But material, much of it yet in the quarry or forest and little of it fully prepared, does not constitute a house. God is not hard pressed. His patience is infinite. Millions and millions have already been called out to be members of this prospective assembly. God is calling yet and will continue to call throughout the gospel dispensation. His mind is fixed on having a General Assembly indeed—a great congregation— "a great multitude that no mail could number, of all nations, and kindreds, and people, and tongues, to stand before the throne, and before the Lamb, clothed with white robes and with palms in their hands."

The time of the constitution of this assembly is at the second coining of Christ and after the resurrection of the dead and the glorification of the bodies of Christians then living. The processes of constitution are clearly set forth in Matt. 25:31-34; 1 Cor. 15:51-54; 1 Thess. 4:13-17; Eph. 5:27; Rev. 21:2-9.

It has now indeed become a church—a glorious church, or church in glory to be presented to himself as a bride without spot, wrinkle, or any such thing. When he comes he will be glorified in his saints and admired in all them that believe.

That *ecclesia,* like the one on earth, will be both visible and spiritual. "I will show thee the bride, the Lamb's wife," says the angel to John.

Recurring to the figure of a house, Rev. 21 and 22 exhibit it as at last completed and occupied. At last completed God himself inhabits it, for says the Scripture, "Behold the tabernacle of God is with men, and he shall be with them, and they shall be his people, and God himself shall be with them and be their God. And God shall wipe away all tears from their eyes; and there shall be no more death, neither sorrow, nor crying, neither shall there be any more pain; for the former things are passed away." Mark that, brethren, "The former things are passed away." Former and latter things are not co-existent. The tabernacle of the wilderness passes away for the more glorious temple of Solomon. The temple then passes away for the still more glorious church on

Ecclesia — THE CHURCH

earth. In like manner the church on earth must pass away for the infinitely glorious church in heaven. There is a Jerusalem on earth, but the heavenly Jerusalem is above. It is free, and the mother of all the saved. But, brother, the general assembly is not yet. The church on earth, the house that Jesus has already built, the house of the living God, which is the pillar and ground of the truth—*this house has the right of way just now.* It is the only existing assembly. Honor the house that now is.

Quite naturally, if tabernacle and temple had been co-existent, one then living would have preferred the temple and discredited the tent.

Equally so if the particular assembly and general assembly are now co-existent, side by side on earth, could you seriously blame a man for resting content with membership in the greater and more honorable assembly?

But as the Scriptures represent these two assemblies, one existing now on earth, the other prospective in heaven, if a man on earth and in time, not qualified by either sanctification of spirit or glorification of body for the heavenly assembly, shall despise membership in the particular assembly because claiming membership in the General Assembly, is not his claim both an absurdity and a pretext? Does he not hide behind it to evade honoring God's existing institution, and the assuming of present responsibilities and the performing of present duties? Yet again, if one believes that there are co-existent on earth and in time, two churches, one only visible and formal, the other real, invisible and spiritual, is there not danger that such belief may tend to the conviction that the form, government, polity and ordinances of the inferior church are matters of little moment? Has not this belief oftentimes in history done this very thing? And is it not an historical fact that, since Protestant Pedo-baptists invented this idea of a now-existing, invisible, universal, spiritual church, to offset the equally erroneous Romanist idea of a present visible, universal church, reverence and honor for God's New Testament particular church have been ground to fine powder between them as between the upper and nether millstones? Today when one seeks to obtain due honor for the particular assembly, its ordinances, its duties, is he not in many cases thwarted in measure, or altogether in some cases, by objections arising from one or the other of these erroneous views?

And when some, endeavoring to hedge against the manifest errors of both these ideas, have invented middle theories to the effect that the church on earth is composed either of all *professing* Christians living at one time, considered collectively, or of all *real* Christians so living and so considered, or of all existing denominations considered as branches of which the church is the tree, have they not multiplied both the absurdities and the difficulties by their assumed liberality of compromise?

Finally, replying to some of your questions:

1. When our Lord says, "On this rock I will build my church and the gates of hell shall not prevail against it," does he refer to the church on earth or to the church in glory?

My answer is, to the particular assembly on earth, considered as an *institution*. The church in glory will never be in the slightest danger of the gates of hell. Before it becomes an assembly, both death and hell, gates and all, are cast into the lake of fire (Rev. 20:14 and 21:4). It is the church on earth that is in danger, from the fear of which this glorious promise is a guaranty.

2. Does your idea of "a general assembly" depend exclusively upon that phrase of doubtful application in Hebrews 12:23, which many good scholars, including prominent Baptists, construe with "myriads of angels" instead of with "the church of the First Born?"

Certainly not. Though I myself strongly hold with our

Ecclesia — THE CHURCH

English versions in referring both the *panegyros* (general assembly) and the *ecclesia* (church) of that passage to saved men and not to angels. The idea of general assembly is clearly in other passages as Eph. 5:25-27; Rev. 7:9 and 21:24.

3. If the figures, '"body" and "bride," apply to each particular church, does not that teach that Christ has many bodies, many brides?

My answer is, first, that your objection, or supposed difficulty, lies not against my view, but against the express teaching of many Scriptures. What the Scriptures teach is true, and difficulties and objections may take care of themselves. But, second, the objection is specious and the difficulty only apparent, since each particular assembly is *a representation or type* of the general assembly, and therefore the broadest figures of the antitype may be applied to all its types without being obnoxious to the criticism. There may well be many representations of the body or bride of Christ.

4. Do you dis-fellowship your Baptist brethren who teach the present existence of "an universal, invisible, spiritual church?"

Most certainly not, so long as they duly honor the particular assembly and its ordinances, as multitudes of them do, in spite of the natural tendency of their theory to discredit it. Many of them, known to me personally, are devoted to the particular church and its ordinances, responsibilities and duties. I delight to honor, fellowship and love these men. We agree that all the redeemed will constitute the general assembly, and that *then* it will be the real body, bride, temple, flock and house of God. We differ as to the co-existence of the two assemblies. They say both now. I say the particular now and the general hereafter.

It will take a wider divergence than this to make me dis-fellowship a Baptist brother, though I honestly and strongly hold that even on this point his theory is erroneous and tends practically to great harm. Yes, I do most emphatically hold that this theory is responsible for incalculable dishonor put upon the church of God on earth. I repeat that the theory of the co-existence, side by side, on earth of two churches of Christ, one formal and visible, the other real, invisible and spiritual, with different terms of membership, is exceedingly mischievous and is so confusing that every believer of it becomes muddled in running the lines of separation. Do let it sink deep in your minds that the tabernacle of Moses had the exclusive right of way in its allotted time and the temple of Solomon had the exclusive right of way in its allotted time — so the church of Christ on earth, the particular assembly, now has the exclusive right of way, and is without a rival on earth or in heaven—and so the general assembly in glory, when its allotted time arrives, will have exclusive right of way.

Had I lived in the days of Moses I would have given undivided honor to the tabernacle—in the days of Solomon to the Temple alone—and when the general assembly comes, that shall be my delight. But living now I must honor the house that Jesus built. It is the house of the living God, the pillar and ground of the truth. To it are committed the oracles and promises of God. To it is given the great commission. It is the instructor of angels and in it throughout all the ages of time is the glory of God. If I move out of this house, I must remain houseless until Jesus comes. It is the only church you can join in time.

5. What is the distinction, if any, between the kingdom and the church?

My answer is that the kingdom and church on earth are not co-terminus. Kingdom, besides expressing a different idea, is much broader in signification than a particular assembly or than all the particular assemblies. The particular church is that executive institution or business body, within the kingdom, charged with official duties and responsibilities for the spread of the kingdom.

Ecclesia — THE CHURCH

In eternity and glory church and kingdom may be co-terminus. Like the church, the kingdom in both time and eternity has both visible and spiritual aspects.

6. As a sufficient reply to several other questions:

Let it be noted that this discussion designedly avoids applying certain adjectives to the noun "church," not merely because the New Testament never applies them to *Ecclesia,* but because they are without distinguishing force when contrasting the particular assembly with the general assembly.

For example: "Local," "visible," "spiritual."

Locality inheres in *Ecclesia.* There can be no assembly now or hereafter without *a place to meet.* When existing in fact, both the particular assembly in time, and the general assembly in eternity, are both visible and spiritual. Why attempt to distinguish by terms which do not distinguish?

Katholikos (Catholic or Universal) is not a New Testament word at all and hence is never applied by inspiration to *Ecclesia.* Nor is it a Septuagint word at all.

In post-apostolic times it crept without authority into the titles of certain New Testament letters, as "The First Epistle General (*Katholikos*) of Peter." And even there it could not mean "universal," since Peter, himself, four times limits his address:

(a) First to *Jews* (not Gentiles.)

(b) Then to "elect" Jews (not all Jews.)

(c) Then to elect Jews of the *Dispersion* (not to Jewish Christians in Palestine.)

(d) Then to elect Jews of the Dispersion in "Pontes, Galatia, Cappadocia, Asia and Bithynia," *i.e.,* the comparatively small district of Asia Minor (not in the rest of Asia, Europe and Africa.) Neither in the sense of every place, nor of every person in the universe, can the English word "universal" be applied to *Ecclesia*.

7. Certain other questions must be deferred to a subsequent lecture, namely

(a) Did our Lord purpose and provide for the perpetuity of the church on earth as an *institution* until his second advent?

(b) Can this perpetuity be traced historically?

Also, in subsequent lectures will be considered the other questions of our lesson, namely: Who established the church and when, What its foundation, What the gates of hell, Signification of the keys, and of binding and loosing.

APPENDIX NO. 1

The object of this appendix is to enable the country preacher with few books, and who knows nothing of Greek, to form his own conclusions as to the meaning of *ecclesia,* based upon an inductive study of the usage of the word. A few instances only are cited from the classics, out of the great number read to my class in second lecture, but enough for the purpose. These citations will be particularly helpful in showing the distinction between the particular *ecclesia,* or business body of even the smallest Greek state, and *panegyros,* (general, festive assembly) when the people of all the Greek states assembled. By this means even an uneducated preacher may understand the fitness of calling the great heavenly gathering in glory, the "General Assembly and Church of the first-born" *(panegyros kai ecclesia)* in contra-distinction to the particular business assembly on earth.

The New Testament usage is given entire because so few country preachers have the Englishmen's Greek Concordance.

The Septuagint usage is also given entire so far as the Trommius Concordance (A.D. 1718) cites instances. This usage is regarded as particularly valuable for three reasons:

(1) Only about one preacher in a thousand has access to a Septuagint concordance.

(2) Nearly all their ideas of the meaning of the word in the Greek Old Testament have been derived from the loose generalizations of the great Pædobaptist scholars. Harnack, Hatch, Hort, Cremer, *et al, who* seeing that *ecclesia* sometimes translates the Hebrew word *"qahal,"* foist upon *ecclesia* all the meanings of *qahal* in other connections. You have nothing to do with *qahal* except where *ecclesia* translates it.

By an inductive study of all the *ecclesia* passages, you will see for yourselves that in the Septuagint it never means "all Israel whether assembled or unassembled," but that *in every instance* it means a gathering together, an assembly.

(3) This classic, and particularly this Septuagint usage, are specially valuable to you, because as the first lecture states, the mew Testament writers neither. coined this word nor employed it in an unusual sense. The apostles and early Christians were more familiar with the Septuagint than with the Hebrew Version. From it they generally quoted. They wrote in Greek to a Greek-speaking world, and used Greek words as a Greek-speaking people would understand them.

It is a fiction of Pædobaptists that they used *"baptizo" in a* new and sacred sense. Equally is it a fiction that *Ecclesia* was used in any new, special sense. The object of Christ's *ecclesia,* and terms of membership in it, were indeed different from those the classic or Septuagint *ecclesia*. But the word itself retains its ordinary meaning. In determining this meaning we look to the common, literal usage. If occasionally we find it used in a general or figurative way, these few instances must be construed in harmony with the common, literal signification.

USAGE IN THE CLASSICAL GREEK

Ecclesia. Primary meaning: An organized assembly of citizens, regularly summoned, as opposed to *other meetings.*

Thucydides 2,22:—"Pericles, seeing them angry at the present state of things * * did not call them to an assembly *(ecclesia)* or any other meeting."

Demosthenes 378,24:—"When after this the assembly *(ecclesia)* adjourned, they came together and planned * * For the future still being uncertain, meetings and speeches of all sorts took place in the market-place. They were afraid that an assembly *(ecclesia)* would be summoned suddenly, etc." Compare the distinction here between a lawfully assembled business body and a mere gathering together of the people in unofficial capacity, with the town-clerk's statement in Acts 19:33-40.

Now some instances of the particular *ecclesia* of the several Greek states—

Thucydides 1,87:—"Having said such things, he himself, since he was ephor, put the question to vote in the assembly *(ecclesia)* of the Spartans."

Thucydides 1,139:—"And the Athenians having made a house (or called an assembly, *ecclesia*) freely exchanged their sentiments."

Aristophanes Act. 169:—"But I forbid you calling an assembly *(ecclesia)* for the Thracians about pay."

Thucydides 6,8:—"And the Athenians having convened an assembly *(ecclesia)* ** voted, etc."

Thucydides 6,72:—"And the Syracusans having buried their dead, summoned an assembly (*ecclesia*).

This historical reading concerning the business assemblies of the several petty but independent, self-governing Greek states, with their lawful conference, their free speech, their decision by vote, whether of Spartans, Thracians, Syracusans or Athenians, sounds much like the proceedings of particular and independent Baptist churches to-day.

Panegyros—A general, festive assembly of the people of all the Greek states.

Decret. ap Demos: 526,16—"Embassies to the festal assemblies *(panegyros)* in Greece."

Plato, Hipp. 363: —"Going up to Olympia, the festal assemblies *(panegyros) of* the Greeks."

Pindar:—"The General Assembly *(panegyros)* in honor of Zeus (Jupiter)."

Isocrates 41 A: —"I often wondered at those who organized the general festivals *(panegyros)."*

Aeschylus Theb. 220:—"May this goodly, general company *(panegyros)* of gods never fail the city in my life time."

Thucydides 5,50:—"And fear was produced in the General Assembly *(panegyros)* that the Lacedæmonians would come in arms." Upon this usage note how bright and discriminating the Greek mind.

This General Assembly was not for war but peace. Let not the Spartans come to it with arms in their hands. It was not for business, but pleasure—a time of peace, and joy and glory.

In the happy Greek conceit, all the heavenly beings were supposed to be present. How felicitously does an inspired apostle adapt himself to the Greek use of the word, and glorify it by application to the final heavenly state. God the judge, not Zeus, is there. Myriads of angels, not Greek demigods and inferior deities, are there.

There is a General Assembly in magnitude, multitude and constituency, transcendently above the poor limitations of a small Greek nation—this is made up of every tribe and tongue and kindred, Jew, Roman, Greek, barbarian, Scythian, bond and free. Here warfare is over and rest has come. Here crowns are awarded, not of fading wreaths of time, but crowns of life, righteousness, joy and glory.

Usage in Septuagint

Cited in the concordance of Abraham Trommius (1718). Chapters and verses here given according to Revised Version for Canonical books; and according to Haydock's Douay Bible for *Apochryphal* books.

Greek text used for verification Henry Barclay Sweet — Cambridge 1891.

The *underscored* English word is the translation of *Ecclesia*.

Lev. 8:3—"*Assemble* thou all the congregation."

Here the verb (ecclesiazo) is used. Though Trommius cites a reading which has the noun.

Deut. 18:16—"In the day of the *assembly*." (referring to the convocation at Sinai)

Deut. 23:1, 2, 3, 8—"Shall not enter into the *assembly* of the Lord." Here four times used to proscribe certain specified classes from admission into the Lord's assembly.

Deut. 31:30—"And Moses spoke in the ears of all the *assembly* of Israel the words of this song."

Josh. 5:35 —"Joshua read before all the *assembly* of Israel."

Judges 20:2—"And the chiefs of all the people presented themselves in the *assembly* of the people of God." The place of this assembly was Mizpah.

Judges 21:5—"And the children of Israel said, Who is there among all the tribes of Israel that came not up in the *assembly* unto the Lord."

Judges 21:8—"There came none to the camp from Jabesh-Gilead to the *assembly*."

1 Sam. 17:47—"David said, "That all this *assembly* may know there is a God in Israel."

1 Sam. 19:20—"And when Saul's messenger saw the *company* of the prophets prophesying."

1 Kings 8:14, 22, 55, 65—"Blessed all the *congregation*"—"in the presence of all the congregation"—"blessed all the *congregation*"—"and all Israel with him, a great *congregation*."

1 Chron. 13:2, 4—"David said unto all the *assembly* of Israel"—"and all the *assembly* said."

1 Chron. 28:2—"David stood up upon his feet—(in the midst of the *assembly*)". Nothing in Hebrew text for the words in parenthesis, and hence nothing in English version.

1 Chron. 28:8—"In the sight of all Israel, the *congregation* of the Lord."

1 Chron. 29:1—"The King said unto all the *congregation*."

1 Chron. 29:10—"David blessed the Lord before all the *congregation*."

1 Chron. 29:20—"David said to all the *congregation*."

2 Chron. 1:3, 5—"Solomon, and all the *congregation* with him." "Solomon and the *congregation* sought unto it." (the altar)

2 Chron. 6:3, 12, 13—"The King turned his face and blessed all the *congregation*." "he stood * * in the presence of all the *congregation*." "He kneeled down * * before all the *congregation*."

2 Chron. 7:8—"Solomon held the feast * * and all Israel with him, a very great *congregation*."

2 Chron. 29:5, 14—"Jehosaphat stood in the *congregation*." Then upon Jahaziel * * came the spirit of the Lord in the midst of the *congregation*."

2 Chron. 23:3—"And all the *congregation* made a covenant

Ecclesia — THE CHURCH

with the King."

2 Chron. 28:14—"So all the armed men left all the captives and the spoil before the princes and all the *congregation*."

2 Chron. 29:23, 32—"And they brought the sin offering before the king and the *congregation*" "And the number of the burnt offerings which the *congregation* brought."

2 Chron. 30:2, 4, 13, 17, 23, 24, 25—"The King, his princes and all the *congregation*." "In the eyes of the King and all the *congregation*." "A very great *congregation*." "Many in the *congregation* who had not sanctified themselves." "And the *congregation* took counsel." "Hezekiah did give to the *congregation*." "And all the *congregation*."

Ezra 2:64—"The whole *congregation* together was 42,360."

Ezra 10:1—"There was gathered together a very great *congregation*."

Ezra 10:9—"That whosoever came not within three days * * should be himself separated from the *congregation* of the captivity."

Ezra 10:12—"Then all the *congregation* answered."

Ezra 10:14—"Let * * rulers of the *congregation* stand." (Sinaiatic)

Neh. 5:7—"And I held a great *assembly* against them."

Neh. 5:13—"And all the *congregation* said Amen."

Neh. 7:66—"The whole *congregation* together was 42,360."

Neh. 8:2—"Ezra brought the law before the *congregation*."

Neh. 8:17—"And all the *congregation* of them * * made booths."

Neh. 13:1—"An ammonite and Moabite shall not enter the *congregation*."

Job. 39:28—"I stand up in the *assembly* and cry for help."

Psa. 22:22—"In the midst of the *congregation* will I praise."

Psa. 22:25—"Of thee cometh my praise in the great *congregation*."

Psa. 26:5—"I have hated the *congregation* of evildoers."

Psa. 26:12—"In the *congregations* will I bless the Lord."

Psa. 35:18—"I will give thee thanks in the great *congregation*."

Psa. 49:9—"I have published the righteousness in the great *congregation*."

Psa. 68:26—"Bless ye God in the *congregations*."

Psa. 89:5—"Thy faithfulness in the *assembly* of the holy ones."

Psa. 107:32—"Let them exalt him in the *assembly* of the people."

Psa. 149:1—"Sing his praise in the *assembly* of the saints."

Prov. 5:14—"In the midst of the *congregation* and assembly."

Jer. 31:8—"A great *assembly*" —Instead of *company* is a variant reading.

Lam. 1:10—"They should not enter into the congregation."

Ezek. 32:3—"Here Codex A has *assembly (ecclesia)* instead of "company."

Joel 2:16—"Sanctify the *congregation*."

Micah 2:5—"Cast the line by lot in the *congregation* of the Lord."

Usage in the Apocrypha

Judith:

Judith 6:2—"Ozias took him from the *assembly* to his house."

Judith 7:29—"Great weeping in the *assembly*."

Judith 13:29—"In the *assembly* of the people."

Judith 14:6—"Saw the head of Holofernes in the hand of one of the *assembly*." (A reading)

Ecclesiasticus:

Ecclesiasticus 15:5—"In the midst of the *assembly* she shall open his mouth."

Ecclesiasticus 21:20—"The mouth of the prudent is sought after in the *assembly*."

Ecclesiasticus 23:34—"This woman shall be brought into the *assembly*."

Ecclesiasticus 24:2—"Wisdom shall open her mouth in the *assemblies* of the Most High."

Ecclesiasticus 26:6—"My heart hath been afraid of the *assembly* of the people."

Ecclesiasticus 31:11—"And the assembly shall declare his alms."

Ecclesiasticus 33:19—"Hear me ye rulers of the *assembly*."

Ecclesiasticus 38:37—"They shall not go up to the *assembly*."

Ecclesiasticus 39:14—"The *assembly* shall show forth his praise."

Ecclesiasticus 44:15 "Let the *assembly* declare his praise."

Ecclesiasticus 50:15—"before all the *assembly of* Israel."

Ecclesiasticus 50:22—"lifted up his hands over all the *assembly* of the children of Israel."

1 MACCABEES:

1 Maccabees 2:56—"Caleb for bearing witness before the *congregation*."

1 Maccabees 3:13—"Judas had assembled *a company* of the faithful."

1 Maccabees 4:59—"Judas, his brethren and all the *assembly*."

1 Maccabees 5:16—"A great *assembly* met."

1 Maccabees 14:19—"read before the *assembly* in Jerusalem."

Ecclesia — THE CHURCH

REMARK ON SEPTUAGINT USAGE

The testimony here is univocal. It is as solid as the Macedonian phalanx. Some have tried to make it appear that four of these ninety-two instances refer to an unassembled *ecclesia*. Look at them, read the context and judge for yourselves. The four passages are: 1 Kings 8:65; 1 Chron. 28:8; Ezra 10:8; Ezek. 32:3. The first two settle themselves.

In Ezra "the assembly of the Captivity" simply Means the 42,360 that returned from the captivity and are repeatedly gathered together.

In Ezek. 32:3 an unreliable reading has *ecclesia* in the place of *company*. But whether company or *ecclesia,* the idea is the same. The "many peoples" signify nothing, they do not constitute an *ecclesia* until formed into one company. Xerxes, Timour, *Napoleon and* many others formed one great company out of the contingents of many nations.

Observe prescribed conditions of membership in Deut. 23 and Neh. 13.

The new and mammoth Septuagint Concordance of Hatch and Redpath, five folio volumes, Oxford, 1893, gives the following additional instances (not cited by Trommius) from one text or another:

CANONICAL BOOKS.

Deut. 4:10; 9:10; 1 Kings 1:3 (from Codex A.); Chron. 10:3; 29:28, 31; 30:25; all rendered *assembly* in our Revised Version, and Ezek. 32:23 (from Codex A.) rendered *company*.

APOCHRYPHAL BOOKS.

Judith 6:19, 21, *assembly*.

1 Maccabees 14:9 (assemblies instead of streets).

FROM OTHER GREEK VERSIONS OF OLD TESTAMENT.

Lev. 4:14, 21; 16:17; Psa. 40:9, 10; Prov. 26:26 Jer. 26:17; 44:14. All rendered *assembly* in our Revised Version. And Ezek. 23:47; 26:7; 27:27; 32:22, all rendered *company*.

This makes the Old Testament usage amount to about 114 cases, nearly equal in number to New Testament usage. In no one of the 114 instances does it mean an unassembled *ecclesia*.

USAGE IN THE NEW TESTAMENT (COMMON VERSION)

Matt. 16:18—"I will build my *church*."

Matt. 18:17—"tell (it) unto the *church:* but if he neglect to hear the church."

Acts 2:47—"the Lord added to the *church* daily."

Acts 5:11—"fear came upon all the *church*."

Acts 7:38—"he, that was in the *church*."

Acts 8:1—"the *church* which was at Jerusalem."

Acts 8:3—"He made havoc of the *church*,"

Acts 9:31—"Then had the *churches* rest."

Acts 11:22—"the *church* which was in Jerusalem."

Acts 11:26—"assembled themselves with the *church*."

Acts 12:1—"to vex certain of the *church*."

Acts 12:5—"without ceasing of the *church* unto God."

Acts 13:1—"Now there were in the *church*."

Acts 14:23—"elders in every *church,* and had" —

Acts 14:27—"had gathered the *church* together."

Acts 15:2—"on their way by the *church*."

Acts 15:4 —"they were received of the *church*."

Acts 15:22—"elders, with the whole church."

Acts 15:11—"confirming the *churches*."

Acts 16:5—"so were the *churches* established."

Acts 18:22—"gone up, and saluted the church."

Acts 19:32—"for the *assembly* was confused."

Acts 19:39 —"determined in a lawful *assembly*."

Acts 19:41—"thus spoken, lie dismissed the *assembly*."

Acts 20:17—"called the elders of the *church*."

Acts 20:28—"to feed the *church* of God."

Rom. 16:1—"is a servant of the *church*."

Rom. 16:4—"all the *churches* of the Gentiles."

Rom. 16:5—"the church that is in their house."

Rom. 16:16—"The *churches* of Christ salute you."

Rom. 16:23—"mine host, and of the whole *church*."

1 Cor. 1:2—"Unto the *church* of God which"

1 Cor. 4:17—"I teach everywhere in every *church*."

1 Cor. 6:4—"least esteemed in the *church*."

1 Cor. 7:17—"so ordain I in all *churches*."

1 Cor. 10:32—"nor to the *church* of God."

1 Cor. 11:16—"neither the *churches* of God."

1 Cor. 11:18—"come together in the *church*."

7 Cor. 11:22—"or despise ye the *church* of God."

1 Cor. 12:28—"God hath set some in the *church*."

1 Cor. 14:4—"that prophesieth edifieth the *church*."

1 Cor. 14:5—"the *church* may receive edifying."

1 Cor. 14:12—"to the edifying of the *church*."

Ecclesia — THE CHURCH

1 Cor. 14:19—"in the *church* I had rather speak."

1 Cor. 14:23—"The whole *church* be come together."

1 Cor. 14:28—"keep silence in the *church.*"

1 Cor. 14:33—"as in all *churches of* the saints."

1 Cor. 14:34—"keep silence in the *churches.*"

1 Cor. 14:35—"for women to speak in the *church.*"

1 Cor. 15:9—"I persecuted the *church of* God."

1 Cor. 16:1—"to the churches of Galatia."

1 Cor. 16:19—"The *churches* of Asia salute you." —"with the *church* that is in their house."

2 Cor. 1:1—"unto the church of God which."

2 Cor. 8:1—"on the *churches* of Macedonia."

2 Cor. 8:18—"gospel throughout all the *churches.*"

2 Cor. 8:19—"was also chosen of the *churches.*"

2 Cor. 8:23—"the messengers of the "churches."

2 Cor. 8:24—"to them, and before the *churches*

2 Cor. 11:8—"I robbed other *churches,* taking."

2 Cor. 11:28—"the care of the *churches.*"

2 Cor. 12:13 —"were inferior to the *churches.*"

Gal. 1:2—"unto the *churches* of Galatia."

Gal. 1:13—"I persecuted the *church* of God."

Gal. 1:22—"unto the *churches of* Judea."

Eph. 1:22—"gave him (to be) the head over all (things) to the *church.*"

Eph. 3:10 —"might be known by the *church.*"

Eph. 3:21—"glory in the *church* by Christ Jesus."

Eph. 5:23—"Christ is the head of the *church.*"

Eph. 5:24—"the *church is* subject unto Christ."

Eph. 5:25—"as Christ also loved the *church.*"

Eph. 5:27—"to himself a glorious *church.*"

Eph. 5:29—"even as the Lord the *church.*"

Eph. 5:32—"concerning Christ and the *church.*"

Phil. 3:6—"Concerning zeal, persecuting the *church.*"

Phil. 4:15—"no *church* communicated with me."

Col. 1:18—"the head of the body, the *church.*"

Col. 1:24—"body's sake, which is the *church.*"

Col. 4:15—"the *church* which is in the house."

Col. 4:16 —"in the *church* of the Laodiceans."

1 Th. 1:1—"unto the *church* of the Thessalonians."

1 Th. 2:14—"followers of the *churches* of God."

2 Th. 1:1—"unto the *churches* of the Thessalonians."

2 Th. 1:4—"in you in the *churches* of God."

1 Tim. 3:5 —"take care of the *church* of God."

1 Tim. 3:15—"the *church* of the living God."

1 Tim. 5:16—"let not the *church* be charged."

Philem. 2—"to the *church* in the house."

Heb. 2:12—"in the midst of the *church.*"

Heb. 12:23—"*assembly* and *church* of the first born."

Ecclesia — THE CHURCH

Jas. 5:14—"call for the elders of the *church.*"

3 John 6—"the charity before the *church.*"

3 John 9—"I wrote unto the *church.*"

3 John 10—"casteth (them) out of the *church.*"

Rev. 1:4—"John to the seven *churches.*"

Rev. 1:11—"unto the seven *churches* which."

Rev. 1:20—"the angels *of* the seven *churches.*"—"are the seven *churches.*"

Rev. 2:1—"the angel of the *church* of Ephesus."

Rev. 2:7—"the Spirit said unto the *churches.*"

Rev. 2:8—"the angel of the *church* in Smyrna."

Rev. 2:11—"the spirit with unto the *churches.*"

Rev. 2:12—"to the angel of the *church* in Pergamos."

Rev. 2:17—"the Spirit with unto the *churches.*"

Rev. 2:18—"the angel of the *church* in Thyatira."

Rev. 2:23—"all the *churches* shall know."

Rev. 2:29—"the Spirit with unto the *churches.*"

Rev. 3:1—"angel of the *church in* Sardis."

Rev. 3:6—"the Spirit with unto the *churches.*"

Rev. 3:7—"to the angel of the *church* in."

Rev. 3:13—"the Spirit with unto the *churches.*"

Rev. 3:14—"the angel of the *church* of the Laodiceans."

Rev. 22:16—"these things in the *churches.*"

B.H. Carroll

Remark on the New Testament Usage.

Only four of these passages present any difficulty in either classification or exposition, namely: Acts 9:31 (R.V.); Eph. 1:22; Col. 1:18, 24, and these with "flock" in John 10:16, and "house" in Pet. 2:5, are considered in Lecture 2.

ECCLESIA—THE CHURCH.

LECTURE 2.

Questions About the Etymology and Usage of the Greek Word Ecclesia

IT was not the original purpose to extend the discussion of the question, What is the Church, into a second lecture. It was supposed that you would be able of yourselves to classify all New Testament uses of ecclesia under the several heads of abstract, generic, particular and prospective, by applying the principles of the first lecture.

But the nature and variety of your new questions constrain me to enlarge the discussion somewhat and to supply you with a wider usage of the word than the New Testament affords. Of the great number of instances from the classics, read to you, at my request, by Mr. Ragland, our Professor of Greek, your attention is recalled to a few, specially pertinent.

(1) Those which so clearly show the distinction between ecclesia as an organized business body and all unofficial gatherings, e.g., "Pericles seeing them angry at the present state of things—did not call them to in *ecclesia* or any other meeting"—*Thucydides*.

Again, "When after this the *ecclesia* adjourned, they came together and planned for the future still being uncertain, *meetings* and speeches of *all sorts* took place in the market. They were afraid the *ecclesia* would be summoned. Compare this distinction with the town-clerk's statement in Acts 19:39, 40.

(2) Those concerning the *ecclesias* of the several petty but independent Greek states, Sparta, Athens and others, bringing out clearly the business character of these assemblies, their free and democratic deliberations, their final decisions by vote, and reminding us so forcibly of the proceedings of independent Baptist churches of our day.

(3) Those showing the discriminating character of the Greek mind in the use of *panegyros,* as distinguished from *ecclesia.*

Ecclesia was the particular and independent business assembly of any Greek state, however *small. Panegyros* was the General Assembly of the people of all the Greek states. It was a festive assembly looking to rest, joy, peace, glory, and not to business and war. Let not the Lacedaemonians come up armed to this assembly.

It was a happy Greek conceit that all the Heavenly beings were present at these Olympian meetings. How felicitously does the inspired author of the letter to the Hebrews adapt himself to this discrimination, when in contrast with the particular *ecclesia* on earth, he writes of the General Assembly and church of the first born in glory—*panegyros kai ecclesia.* There, not Zeus, but God the judge. There not a pantheon of inferior deities and demi-gods, but myriads of angels, and the spirits of just men made perfect. There war and toil have ceased, and peace and rest reign forever. There are bestowed not fading laurels, but everlasting crowns of life, righteousness, joy and glory (See 1 Cor. 9:25; 2 Tim. 4:8; James 1:12; 1 Pet. 5:4; Rev. 2:10; 9:7).

That General Assembly is not bound by the limitations of the one Greek nation but infinitely transcends the Olympian gatherings in a countless multitude out of every nation, tribe tongue and kindred. Jew, Greek, Roman, Scythian, barbarian, bond and free mingle in one tide of brotherhood.

Ecclesia — THE CHURCH

Rev. 7:9.

SEPTUAGINT USAGE.

Some of your questions induced me to supply you with the entire Septuagint usage. You have before you now all the instances of this use of *ecclesia,* including the readings of the several texts, in both the canonical books and Apocrypha. To these have been added the additional instances from other Greek versions of the Old Testament, Aquila (A.D. 130), Theodotion (A.D. 160), Symmachus, (A.D. 193) *et al; i.e.*, so far as they are cited in the concordance of Abraham Trommius (A.D. 1718) and the new mammoth concordance of Hatch & Redpath, Oxford (1893). These instances, about 114 in all, nearly equal the dew Testament number, giving us a total of about 230 uses of the word not counting the classics. This is every way *sufficient* for inductive study. Of course the post-apostolic versions of Aquila, Theodotion and Symmachus had no influence in determining the earlier New Testament usage, but as the work of Jews in the second century they confirm that usage.

It was to the classic and Septuagint usage the first lecture referred in saying that the New Testament writers neither coined the word nor employed it in an unusual sense.

They wrote in Greek, to readers and speakers of Greek, using Greek words in their common acceptation in order to be understood. With this usage before us let us seek an answer to your new questions

I. As in the Septuagint *ecclesia* translates the Hebrew word *qahal,* does it not mean "All Israel, whether assembled or unassembled?"

My reply is, I see not how this question could have risen in any mind from a personal, inductive study of all the Septuagint passages, since in every instance of the 114 cited the word means a gathering together—an assembly.

You can see that for yourselves by the context of your

English version. The Septuagint usage is as solidly one thing as the Macedonian phalanx. Unfortunately in our broad theological reading our minds become so preoccupied with the loose generalizations of the great Pedobaptist scholars, Harnack, Hatch, Hort, Cremer and others, that we unconsciously neglect to investigate and think for ourselves. Let not admiration for distinguished scholarship blot out your individuality. Accept nothing blindly on mere human authority.

In determining this question, have nothing to do with the meaning of *qahal* in its other connections. Rigidly adhere to the passages where *ecclesia* translates it. Because a word sometimes serves for another, do not foist on it all the meanings of the other word.

It is well enough to illustrate by synonyms, but do not define by them. Definition by supposed synonyms was the curse of the Baptismal controversy because a question about *purifying* arose between a Jew and John's disciples, Edward Beecher must write in illogical book to show that *Baptizo* means only to *purify,* and, of course, by and method. Study Carson on Baptism and you will learn much about the principles of accurate definition.

II. "But," another question asks, "do not some of these *Septuagint* passages justify the meaning of *unassembled?"*

While I accepted Pedobaptist ideas, I thought so, but never since I looked into the matter for myself. I do not now know of even one such passage. I never heard of a definite claim being set up to more than four out of 114. Turn now to these four in your revised English Bibles. They are 1 Kings 8:65; 1 Chron. 28:8; Ezra 10:8; Ezek. 32:3.

The first two settle themselves by a mere reading. In Ezra "the *assembly* of the captivity" might be supposed to refer, in a loose way, to the people while captives in Babylon. But in fact it has no such reference as the context shows. It simply

⇥ *Ecclesia* — The Church ⇤

means the 42,360 who returned from captivity as a definite Jerusalem assembly, repeatedly called together. In Ezekiel 32:3, an unreliable reading has *ecclesia* for the English word *company*. But even then the idea is the same. "Many peoples" in that sentence signify nothing against the usual meaning of the word.

These do not constitute an *ecclesia* until gathered into a company. Xerxes, Timour, Napoleon, the White Tzar, and many others have formed a great company out of the contingents of many people.

Heretofore the advocates of the present existence of "an universal, invisible, spirituals unassembled church" have boldly rested their case on the *Septuagint* usage. The premise of their argument was, that the New Testament writers must have used the word in the sense that a Jew accustomed to the Greek Old Testament would understand. A fine premise, by the way. But to save the theory from total collapse some new line of defense must be invented. And that is intimated in your next question:

III. "As Christ was establishing a new institution, widely different from the Greek state *ecclesia,* or the Old Testament *ecclesias,* was not *ecclesia* in the New Testament used in a new, special and sacred sense? Does not the word in the New Testament commonly mean the same as the *Kletoi,* or the called, without reference to either organization, or assembly?"

On many accounts I am delighted with the opportunity to reply to this question. The reply is couched in several distinct observations:

(1) This question demonstrates hopeful progress in the controversy and prophesies a speedy and final settlement. It not only necessarily implies a clean-cut surrender of the old line of defense, but also narrows a hitherto broad controversy into a single new issue, susceptible of easy settlement. If this new position prove untenable there is

no other to which the defense can he shifted. This is the last ditch. And the fact that it is *new* indicates the extremity of its advocates.

(2) Like the former contention, this, too, is borrowed from the Pedobaptists. They tried hard and long to make it serve in the Baptismal controversy. Their contention then was that though *Baptizo* meant to clip or immerse in classic Greek, yet in the Bible it was used in a new and sacred sense. The scholarship of the world rebuked them. Words are signs of ideas. To mean anything they must be understood according to the common acceptation in the minds of those addressed. I know of no more dangerous method of interpretation than the assumption that a word must be taken to mean something different from its real meaning. Revelation in that case ceases to be revelation. We are at sea without helm, or compass, or guiding star.

(3) There is nothing in the difference between Christ's *ecclesia* on the one hand, and the classic or Septuagint *ecclesia* on the other hand, to justify a new sense in the word. The difference lies not in the meaning of the word, but in the object, terms of membership and other things.

(4) This proposed new sense destroys the two essential ideas of the old word, organization and assembly, and thereby leaves Christ without an *institution* or official, *business* body in the world. From the days of Abel the *Kletoi,* or called, have been in the world. It therefore the New Testament *ecclesia* means only the "called," then what did Christ establish in his time?

(5) If by eccles*ia,* only the called in their scattered capacity are meant, why use both *ecclesia* and *Kletoi?*

How can there be a *body of Kletoi* if the essential ideas of *ecclesia* are left out? If there be no organization, no assembly, how can there be a *body?* Miscellaneous, scattered, unattached units do not make a body.

Ecclesia — The Church

(6) Finally there is not the slightest evidence that *ecclesia* has any such arbitrary meaning. But this will more clearly appear if you examine the usage passage by passage.

IV. "But when Paul says, I persecuted the church, surely that can only mean that he persecuted the disciples?"

But it does mean much more. It means exactly what it says. The mere individuals as such counted nothing with Paul. It was the organization to which they belonged, and what that organization stood for. As proof of this our Lord arrested him with the question: "Why persecutest thou me? I am Jesus whom thou persecutest." Jesus was not persecuted in person by Saul.

So when "Herod the King put forth his hand to afflict certain of the church"—he aimed at the organization, in what it stood for, though directly his wrath fell only on James and Peter.

The present cruel assault on Dr. Gambrell, here in Texas, is not so much against J.B. Gambrell, the individual, but against the mighty and peerless exponent of the Convention, its policies, methods and work. It is persecution of the Convention.

V. "But if church means *assembly* does not that require it to be always in session?"

No *ecclesia,* classic, Jewish, or Christian, known to history, held perpetual session. They all adjourned and came together again according to the requirements of the case. The organization, the institution, was not dissolved by temporary adjournment.

VI. "But if the earthly ecclesia exists now, though many of its members forsake the assembling of themselves together, and if it continually receives new members, why may we not say the General Assembly exists now, though all be not actually assembled, nor all its members yet born?"

This is the most plausible objection yet offered, and one that greatly perplexes some minds. Your rigid attention, therefore, is called to the reply. It is admitted that the particular assembly on earth is not always in session either as a worshipping or business body. The word *ecclesia* never did require perpetual session. Nor does it now. There has been no change of requirement in that respect from the days of Pericles till now. Nor does the word require that all its *Kletoi* or members shall be present at every session. Nor does the word itself forbid the accession of new members.

Moreover a particular *ecclesia* might continue as an historic institution so long that there might be an entire change in the *personnel* of its members many times. There are particular Baptist churches now existing in which these changes have actually occurred. Seldom does the roll of members remain the same even one year. Some die, some are excluded, some move away into other communities, new members are received. The attendance upon the sessions for worship and business continually varies. Some are sick, some travel, some backslide. Conditions of weather, politics or war effect the attendance. Yea, more, storms, plagues, or persecution may for the time being scatter the members of a particular church over a wide area of territory. None of these things in the slightest decree affect the meaning of the cord.

Ecclesia remains throughout an organized assembly whose members are properly called out from their private homes or business to attend to public affairs.

The difference between the earthly and heavenly *ecclesia* in regard to the foregoing mutations does not arise at all from the word but from the nature of the case.

By its very nature the earthly *ecclesia* is imperfect. It is a time institution. By the conditions of its earthly existence there are fluctuations in attendance and membership. By its location in a world of lost people and by its commission to

Ecclesia — The Church

save them, there is constant accession of members.

The changed nature of the case and of the conditions make these things different with the *General Assembly*. It can not increase in members because there is no salvable material from which to grin accessions. Character has chrystalized and probation ended. The lost then, are forever lost, and hell admits of no evangelism. The word would not forbid evangelism but the nature of the case does.

Not only the word, but the nature of the case renders present existence of the *General Assembly* impossible. Into the earthly house material enters according to credible evidence of regeneration as men judge. There is no absolute guaranty against self-deception or hypocrisy. Moreover this material even when the profession of faith is well founded, is never in a perfect state, but must be continually made better by progressive sanctification of soul. The earthly *ecclesia* is a workshop in which material is being prepared for the Heavenly house. Death is the last lesson of discipline for the soul. The resurrection and glorification of the body, its last lesson. No rough ashlar goes into the Heavenly House—no unhewn, unpolished, unadorned cedar timber. No half-stone or broken column would be received. If a soul, even one of the spirits of the just made perfect, were now put into that wall, the building would have to be reconstructed and readjusted to admit the body-part of that same living stone after the resurrection. There is no sound of hammer, axe, or chisel when that building goes up. *All preparatory work of every stone in that building, and of every timber, must be completed before that building goes up.*

It was this heavenly *ecclesia*, which as a coming event, cast its shadow before David and Solomon and constituted their inexorable plan for the typical temple. Because the plan given them was a shadow of better things to come they were not allowed to vary a hairs-breadth from the pattern of the Divine Architect.

There is nothing in the word *ecclesia* itself to forbid its application to "the Spirits of the just made perfect" now in heaven and continually receiving accessions. They are an assembly in fact. And Thayer seems to so understand Hebrews 12:23. I do not agree with him in making "General Assembly and church of the firstborn" synonymous with "the spirits of the just made perfect." To my mind they represent two very distinct ideas. But he is certainly right in supposing that the assembled spirits of the righteous dead may be called an *ecclesia*. But when one defines the *General Assembly* to be the aggregate of all the elect, and then affirms its present existence, he does violence to philology, common sense and revelation. The earthly *ecclesia* is an organization now, an assembly now, though not always in session. The General Assembly is not an organization now, is not an assembly now and therefore exists only as a prospect.

VII. You ask for a particular explanation of several Scriptures which seem difficult to harmonize with the contentions of the first lecture, all of which in turn will now receive attention:

(1) Acts 9:31—"So the church throughout all Judea and Galilee and Samaria had peace, being edified; and walking in the fear of the Lord and in the comfort of the Holy Spirit, was multiplied." (P.V.) To my mind this is the only use of *ecclesia* in all Biblical or classic literature that is difficult of explanation. The difficulty is frankly confessed. Nor am I sure that such explanation as I have to offer will be satisfactory to you. In any event nothing is ever gained for truth by lack of candor. Judging from the uniform use of the word elsewhere one would naturally expect here a plural noun with plural verbs as we have in the King James Version.

And this expectation would be entirely apart from a desire to serve a theory. The difficulty here does not help the theory of "the now-existing universal, invisible, spiritual church."

⇥ *Ecclesia* — THE CHURCH ⇤

It is quite easy to explain it so far as and comfort would accrue to that theory. The difficulty lies in another direction entirely, and seems to oppose a Baptist contention on another point, in whose maintenance my Baptist opponents in the present controversy are fully as much concerned as myself. On its face the passage seems to justify the *provincial* or *state-wide* or *national use* of the word church on earth which all Baptists deny. That is the only difficulty I see in the passage. All the context shows that the reference is to the earth church and not to the heavenly. The limits of this lecture forbid a discussion of the text question. The texts vary. Some manuscripts and versions have the very plural noun with its plural verbs that one would naturally expect from the uniform usage elsewhere. The King James Version follows these. The oldest and best manuscripts, however, have the singular noun with corresponding verbs. The revised Version follows them.

Now for the explanation:

(1) The reading. "Churches," followed by the common version may be the right one, leaving nothing to explain. In all other cases, whether in old or new testament, where the sense calls for the plural, we have it in the text. Not to have it here is an isolated, jarring exception. See Acts 15:41; 16:5; Rom.16:4, 6; 1 Cor. 7:17; 11:26; 14:33, 34; 16:1, 19; 2 Cor. 8:1, 18, 23; 11:8, 28; 12:23; Gal. 1:2, 22; 1 Thess. 2:14; 2 Thess. 1:4; Rev. 1:4, 11, 20; 2:7, 11, 17, 20, 23; 3:6, 13, 22; 22:16; Psa. 26:12; 68:26; Ecclesiasticus 24:2. It is well to note that Murdoch's translation of the Petite Syriac cites a Greek plural in the Margin.

(2) But accepting the singular, according to Revised Version, then, says Dr. Broadus, "the word probably denotes the original church at Jerusalem; whose members were by persecution widely scattered throughout Judea and Galilee and Samaria, and held meetings wherever they were, but still belonged to the one original organization.

When Paul wrote to the Galatians, nearly twenty years later, these separate meetings had been organized into distinct churches; and so he speaks (Gal. 1:22), in reference to that same period, of the churches of Judea which were in Christ."—Com. on Matt., p. 359. This was the church which Saul persecuted and of which he made havoc. Concerning the effect of this persecution the record says, "they were scattered abroad throughout the regions of Judea and Samaria,"—Acts 8:1. "Now they who were scattered abroad upon the persecution that arose about Stephen traveled as far as Phenice, and Cyprus, and Antioch, preaching the word"—Acts 11:19. So, when in the paragraph just preceding our Scripture, there is au account of Saul, as a convert, worshipping and preaching with the church he had formerly persecuted, we may not he surprised at the statement, "So the church throughout all Judea and Galilee and Samaria had peace." Meyer says the "So draws an inference from the whole history in vv. 3-30: in consequence of the conversion of the former chief enemy and his transformation into the zealous apostle."

But you may say, when they are thus scattered does not that break up the *assembly* idea in the word? This question has been previously answered in this lecture. It has been said that a storm, like that which swept. Galveston, or a plague, like the yellow fever in Memphis, or war, as during the colossal strife between the states, or persecution, as in this case, might scatter far. and wide, for the time being, the members of a particular church, but that would not change the meaning of the word church. When Tarleton made a dash at the Virginia legislature the members fled in' every direction. When Howe moved on Philadelphia the Continental Congress dispersed and sought rest in safer places, but who would infer from these cases a change of meaning in legislature or congress? Under the advice of Themistocles the entire Athenian *ecclesia* abandoned their sacred city and sought safety from Persian invasion on their ships, but *ecclesia* retained its meaning.

(3) There is a third explanation possible. You may like it better than I do. It is not in harmony with one statement of my first lecture. It certainly, however, excludes comfort from the theory of the invisible general church.

Meyer understands *ecclesia* in Acts 9:31 in a *collective* reuse, not of Christians collectively, but of *churches* collectively. His language is: "Observe, moreover, with the correct reading *ecclesia* (singular number) the aspect of *unity,* under which Luke, surveying *the whole domain of Christendom* comprehends the churches which had been already formed, and were in process of formation."

Note that he says that the *word church* "comprehends the churches," not Christians. Some Baptists follow Meyer. Hooey, in Hackett on Acts, seems to quote Meyer approvingly. This explanation necessarily implies the existence, at this time, of many organized assemblies in Judea, Samaria and Galilee of which we have no definite historic knowledge. True Philip had evangelized the city of Samaria and there was time enough, in the three years since Paul's conversion for forming some churches, if only the record would say as much. If Meyer be right, of course I was wrong in saying that *ecclesia* could not be used in the collective sense of comprehending many particular churches. I do not think he is right, yet the framers of the Amsterdam Confession of English Baptists (1611) seem to adopt this collective sense. After defining the church of Christ to be "a company of faithful people, separated from the world by the word and Spirit of God, being knit unto the Lord, and one unto another, by baptism, upon their own confession of the faith, and sins"—they add in the next article, "That though in respect of Christ the church be one, *yet it consisteth of divers particular congregations,* even so many as there shall be in the world," adding that each particular church, however few in number, is "the body of Christ."

My own explanation is given in (1) and (2). Now, if a theory harmonizes all of 231 uses of a word but one, and gives a possible explanation—of that one the theory is demonstrated.

VIII. The next class of Scriptures which you wish explained is represented by Eph. 1:22, 23; Col. 1:18; 1 Pet. 2:5; Heb. 3:6; John 10:16.

My first remark is that the epistles to the Ephesians and Colossians were circular letters, meant to be read to other churches with equal application. Hence the use of the term church in a more general way than in other letters. The general use, however, does not forbid, but even requires, specific application to and one particular church, as Eph. 2:21, 22, R.V., shows. In like manner Peter's first letter was written to Jewish saints of the dispersion in Asia Minor, but not specifically to and particular church. Hence, when he says; "Ye, also, as living stones are built up a spiritual house," he does not mean that all the Jewish saints in Asia Minor constitute one church. To say the least of it, that is certainly an unbaptistic idea. It also contradicts the record in Acts showing the planting of many particular churches in this section, made up of Jews and Gentiles, and also ignores the seven churches of Revelation, all in the same section. But Peter means, using the word "house" in a generic sense, that whenever and wherever enough of you come together to form a particular church, that will be a spiritual house in which to offer up spiritual sacrifices, acceptable to God through Jesus Christ. Just as in Ephesians 2:21, 22, R.V., the apostle in the same breath converts the general or abstract idea of church into particular churches. Murdock's translation of the Syriac Peshito reads: "And ye also, as living stones, are builded and become spiritual *temples"* in 1 Pet 2:5.

It is characteristic of circular letters to use terms in general form that must find concrete expression in particular forms. A man writing a circular to Texas Baptists at large, or to all Baptist churches of Texas would find it difficult to refrain from using some general expressions which must be left to the common sense of each particular church for making specific application. It is a matter of congratulation that

Ecclesia — The Church

since the *circular,* called the letter to the Ephesians, employs more of these general terms than any other letter, we have been so thoroughly safeguarded from misconstruction of its generalities by three distinct instances of specific application, in Acts 20:28, 29; Eph. 2:21, 22; 1 Tim. 3:14, 15, to this Ephesus church.

The epistle to the Hebrews is even more general in its address than the two just considered and we have only to apply the same principles of interpretation heretofore set forth to understand Heb. 3:6—"Whose house are we." The writer certainly never intended to convey the impression that all Hebrew Christians constituted one church. That also, to say the least of it, is an unbaptistic idea. We know it to be an unscriptural one, because it contradicts Paul in Gal. 1:22. It is utterly illogical to claim either Heb. 3:6 or 1 Pet. 2:5 for examples of the so-called "universal church" idea. If the advocates of this idea insist on denying the particular church in these cases because one letter was addressed to all the Hellenist converts of Asia Minor, and the other was addressed to all the converted Palestinian Hebrews, then I demand that they also stick to the text, and claim for either case Jews and Jews only. This not only shuts them off from the general assembly in which Jew and Gentile form one new man, but forces them to the absurdity of having on earth one Jewish church big as Asia Minor—that big—no more—and the other big as Judea, that big, no more, and that leaves still running at large all the rest of the converted Jews of the dispersion, and puts them in conflict with Scripture history which shows many particular churches in these sections. To show you the difference between the general use of the term "church" in a *circular* of miscellaneous address and its direct and particular use in a document addressed to specific *churches,* compare the use of church in Revelation with the use of church in the letter to the Ephesians. In the twenty times of Revelation we have more than one-sixth of the N.T. usage.

A few words will dispose of John 10:16—"other sheep I have, which are not of this fold: them also I must bring, and they shall hear my voice; and they shall become one flock, one shepherd." This passage is strong confirmation of my first lecture. Considering, the church abstractly, that is, in the sense of au institution, Christ purposed to make of twain, Jew and Gentile, one new man. In each particular church where Jew and Gentile blend, Christ's purpose is partially fulfilled. But in the General Assembly in glory it is completely fulfilled.

When in some of the foregoing Scriptures, Christ is represented as head over all things to the church—his body, you easily meet all the requirements of the language by saying:

(1) He is head over all things to his earth church as an institution.

(2) He is head over all things to any particular earth church.

(3) He is head over all things to his general assembly in glory.

IX. There remain for consideration only two other Scriptures and then all your questions are answered, Eph. 5:25-27; Heb. 12:18-24. And these will receive particular attention because they were cited in the first lecture as referring to the General Assembly.

(1) On Heb. 12:23, you inquire, Does not the tense of the verb "Ye are come * * to the general assembly, etc.," prove the present existence of the general assembly? How else can it be said, ye are come to it?

To which I reply:

In Galatians IV, Paul says that Hagar and Sarah, under an allegory, represent the two covenants. Hagar, or Mt. Sinai, in Arabia, answering to the Jerusalem that *now is,* is the law-covenant gendering to bondage. Sarah, or Mt. Zion,

Ecclesia — The Church

answering to the Jerusalem above, is the grace-covenant gendering to freedom.

So, when in Hebrews XII it says, "Ye are not come unto the mount that might be touched" (*i.e.,* Mt. Sinai), it simply means ye are not under the law covenant, with its threats and horrible outlook. And when it adds, "Ye are come to Mt. Zion, etc.," (perfect tense) it simply means that we are under the grace-covenant with its promises and glorious outlook. In other words, what we have actually reached is a covenant, *a regime,* a standard of life, and are under its requirements and incited by its glorious prospects.

But an exegesis, based on the tense of that verb, which claims that Christians have already attained unto all the alluring elements of the outlook of the grace-covenant, enumerated in that passage, is as *mad as a March hare.*

That Jerusalem is *above,* and because not yet, is contrasted with the Jerusalem that *now is.* It is the city and country set forth in the preceding chapter, toward which the faith and hope of the patriarchs looked. It was a possession to them only in the sense that they were the heirs of a promised inheritance reserved in heaven. Abraham, with the other heirs of that promise, patiently dwelt in tents, "for he looked for a city which hath foundations, whose builder and maker is God." And all the patriarchs "died in faith," *not having received the promises,* but having seen them and greeted them afar off," yea, "and these all, having had witness borne to them through their faith, received not the promise, God having provided some better things for us, that apart from us they should not be made perfect." Heb 11. And so we also (Heb. 12:1) run the race set before us, not yet having attained the goal or received the prize. Compare 1 Cor. 9:25-27; Phil. 3:7-14; 2 Tim. 4:6-8.

Our Lord himself held out the promise, "The pure in heart shall see God." But not yet have we actually come "to God, the judge." But John, in his apocalypse of the Heavenly City, with its general assembly, tells the time of attainment: "And they shall see his face"—Rev. 22:4.

The imagery of Hebrews XII, is that of the Olympic races. A goal marked the terminus of the race. There sat the judge, who, when the races were over, awarded the prize to the victor. In the Christian race the goal is the resurrection and then only comes the prize. (See Phil. 3:7-14 and 1 Tim. 4:6-8.) It is then we come to God the judge who awards the prize.

The example of our Lord is cited, Heb. 12:2, "The joy set before him" was prospective and realized when he sees the travail of his soul and is satisfied.

The angels of that category make unseen visits to us now in our earthly home, but then we shall in fact go to the myriad's of *shining* ones in *their* celestial home.

Now, on earth, with the blood of Christ, our consciences are cleansed from dead works to serve the living God. Put there, we enter the true Holy of Holies, and behold where Jesus, the mediator of the new covenant, did place the blood of sprinkling, that speaketh better things for us than the blood of Abel, on the true Mercy-seat to make atonement for sin. As our *fore-runner,* the Lord, himself, has passed through the veil. But to us, this safe passage, is as yet only a glorious hope, and we "have fled for refuge to lay hold of the hope set before us; which we have as an anchor of the soul, a hope both sure and steadfast"—Heb. 6:17-19.

We, yet in our bodies, have not joined "the spirits of the just made perfect" nor entered "the general assembly and church of the first born, who are written in heaven." When we read Rev. 21 and 22, we sing: "O when, thou city of my God, shall I thy courts ascend!"

(2) Your question on Eph. 5:25-27, is similar. "Verse 29 declares that Christ *nourishes* and *cherishes* the church, as a husband does his wife. Does not this demand the present existence of the general assembly?"

Ecclesia — THE CHURCH

To which I reply:

(1) The nourishing and cherishing of verse 29 refer to after-marriage conduct, as the context shows, and Christ's marriage with the church is far away in the future. (See Rev. 19:7-9; 21:2, 9, 10.)

But let it be misapplied to the prenuptial state—it matters not. The force of any argument in the question is all in the tense of the verbs "nourisheth and cherisheth." Let us turn that argument loose and see what it proves. In the whole passage, Christ and the church come before us under the figures of bride-groom and bride. The church is conceived of as a unit, a person, and all the verbs employed, namely, "loved—gave himself for—might cleanse—might present—nourisheth and cherisheth" follow the requirements of the figure. But when we come to historical facts we find:

(1) That the love, in eternity, preceded the existence of any part of the church.

(2) The giving himself preceded the existence of the greater part of the church.

(3) The cleansing (and the nourishing and cherishing if misapplied) applies to the process of preparing the members, as each in turn comes upon the stage of being throughout the gospel dispensation from Adam to the second advent.

(4) The presentation of the completed and perfected church, as a bride, follows the second advent.

(5) The nourishing and cherishing (rightly applied) of the perfected church, as a wife, follows the presentation.

Now if the present tense of the nourishing proves present existence of the General assembly, does not the past tense of "loved" prove past existence of the general assembly before man was created? Why should the tense of one of the verbs have more proof force in it than another in the same connection? To grant this, however, proves too much and so the argument based on tense is worthless in this case.

Having now devoted an entire lecture to the application of the principles of the first lecture, we may proceed to consider in future lectures the other matters outlined.

SOME COMMENTS ON DR. CARROLL'S LECTURE ON THE CHURCH

The editor of the *Word and Way* writes: "Have read it through. In my opinion you hit the bull's eye square. The publication seems to me especially timely. In the confused condition of the Baptist mind on this question, a wide reading of your lecture will do great good."

From the editors of the *Christian Index* appears the following: "dour position, we think, is entirely correct, and that it is so well fortified that none dare to attack it. We really enjoyed it." Signed, Bell and Graham.

DR. W.C. WILKINSON, of Chicago, Writes: "I have read attentively your lecture on Matt. 16:18, dated Feb., 1903. Certain critical parts of it I have reexamined with care. If there is any way of explaining, in consistency with one another, all the New Testament uses of the word *Ecclesia*, I think you have hit upon that way, which is the same as to say, that I think your views upon the subject are true for it seems irreverent to suppose that Scripture does not admit of being interpreted clearly so as to harmonize with itself throughout. I have been delighted with the lucidity of your exposition as well as with the admirable Christian temper displayed. I have to thank you for throwing what is to me a new light on a much debated, important point of Scripture representation."

REV. J.J. TAYLOR, of Norfolk, Va., writes: "Accept my hearty thanks for your lecture on the Church. With massive and convincing potter you have, stated the truth. Of course you reached these conclusions long before the current agitation began and so it gives me the greater pleasure to find that by my own investigation, which took a certain intensity three or four years ago, I have come into the same views that you hold. The publication of your lecture will go far toward clarifying the atmosphere. The calm and unimpassioned tone, the lucid illustrations and the rigid logic all emanating from one of so eminent influence among us cannot fail to produce a marked effect."

The editor of the *Western Recorder* writes: "I am delighted with it."

PROF. ROBERT N. BARRETT, of Baylor University, writes: "After a critical perusal of your lecture on *Ecclesia*, I can but express my gratification at the satisfactory manner in which the subject is treated and that wholly from an inductive study of the actual passages of Scripture in which the word occurs. The conclusions reached being untrammeled by traditional distinctions of hierarchy and of philosophy. The clear distinction between the visible and invisible, the local and universal conception of church, is the most satisfactory I have seen. It should be embodied in a book on ecclesiology. I think it will contribute much towards clearing away the fog engendered by the controversy now raging between some of our leading papers."

PROF. W.O. CARVER, of the Seminary at Louisville, writes: "Allow me to thank you for a complimentary copy of your lecture *Ecclesia* which I have read with interest. It is vigorous and dignified. I regret to be unable to accept all its processes of reasoning or to agree with its conclusions. None the less have I read it with great interest and high appreciation."

PROF. E.C. DARGAN, of the Seminary at Louisville, writes: "Thank you for sending me your tract on *Ecclesia*. I have glanced through it and will give it a more careful reading later. I have no doubt we are agreed on many of the points involved, and I am more than pleased with the temper, so different from some, in which you write of those who do not go all the way with you."

Appendix No. 2

Baptism in Water

A Discussion of the Lord's Supper

Distinctive Baptist Principles

BAPTISM IN WATER

BAPTISM IN WATER.[1]

THERE was once a wonderful sight. Jerusalem poured forth its thousands to see it. Immense throngs from the surrounding country swelled the tide of sight-seers. They went out to the river Jordan, in which a strangely attired man was administering a new rite for which he was specially commissioned of God. This thronging to the Jordan called forth the question of our Saviour: "What went ye out into the wilderness to see?" The question implied that there was something very striking in the strange man and his mission. The ordinance he administered fixed on him a historical surname (the Baptist) which distinguishes him in all subsequent history. The ordinance thus inaugurated has never lost its attractive power. In every age thousands have stood by rivers, lakes, and pools to witness its symbolism. So this vast throng has gathered now.

To the large number now ready to be baptized, I desire to speak some earnest words of instruction.[2] To you this is a solemn and eventful occasion. That you may understand and joyfully obey the Saviour, now so precious to you, let me commence with his own words. By special appointment, made before his death, the disciples meet him after his resurrection on the designated mountain in far-off Galilee. To them he said

---

[1] Carroll, B.H. *Life Sketch and Sermons.* Comp., J.B. Cranfill. Philadelphia: American Baptist Publication Society, 1893. 293-314.
[2] This sermon was preached to instruct a large number of candidates just before their baptism.

B.H. Carroll

"All power is given unto me in heaven and in earth. Go ye therefore, and teach all nations, baptizing them in the name of the Father, and of the Son, and of the Holy Ghost teaching them to observe all things whatsoever I have commanded you: and, lo, I am with you alway, even unto the end of the world." This closing paragraph of Matthew's Gospel is the great law of baptism. In extent it spans the world to the end of time; and as yonder suspension bridge rests not on intermediate supports but on pillars on opposite shores, so this law rests on the all-prevalent authority which introduces it, and the promised presence which concludes it. As no higher authority can be invoked, and no period of time excepted, and no more potent presence can be promised, the law can never be changed or superseded. What it enjoined is necessarily of perpetual and universal obligation. And as his omniscience looked through all ages, considered all countries and climates, recognized all differences in men, and noted all variations of their condition, so no exception and no exemption and no modification of this law can be claimed by any man, anywhere, under any circumstances that come within the limits of possible obedience. The very order of the several obligations of this law is an essential feature of the law. We may not reverse or transpose these obligations without nullifying the law itself, and incurring the sin of willful and aggravated disobedience. What, then, is the prescribed order of these several obligations? On your consciences, purified by his blood, let me now place them

1. "Make disciples." Pardon me if I call your attention to the fact that "teach" in our English version mis-translates the Greek, *"matheteusate,"* a different word from the "teaching," *didaskontes,* in another clause.

2. "Baptizing them," that is, the discipled.

3. "Teaching them," that is, the baptized disciples, "to observe all things whatsoever I have commanded you."

There is the divine order from which we may not depart

Baptism in Water

without sin. First, make disciples, then baptize the discipled, then instruct the baptized disciples to observe all his other commandments. We may not baptize them before discipling them. We may not require them to observe other ordinances before baptizing them. We may not claim or expect the fulfillment of his promise to be with us alway, unless we do what he has commanded, and as he commanded it. Before examining in detail the import of this divine law of baptism, it will be profitable to fix in your minds a few principles fundamental to the interpretation of any law, and so recognized by all competent authorities.

(1.) The words of a law are to be understood in their plain, ordinary, and popular sense.

(2.) From the words of the law there can be no departure.

(3.) When the law is uncertain, there is no law.

(4.) The expression of one thing is the exclusion of another.

(5.) "It avails little to know what ought to be done, if you do not know how it is to be done."

(6.) "Where anything is commanded, everything by which it is to be accomplished is commanded."

(7.) The law requires absolute obedience. "Obedience is the essence of the law."[3]

(8.) A law to be binding must definitely invest some one with its execution or enforcement.

Bearing these general principles in mind, give me your fixed attention that I may impress on your hearts, indelibly, certain essential features of this great law of baptism

I. To whom was this command given?

---

[3] See J. T. Christian, "Immersion."

Certainly it is addressed to somebody. All laws intended for practical use must charge some one with their execution. A statute is void on its face that makes no provision for its enforcement. It must specify by whom it is to be executed. To whom then did Jesus speak? Certainly not to strangers or enemies. Nor would he commit the ordinances of his kingdom to those who despise and rail at them. Nor would he trust this law of baptism to men who would speak slightingly of it, or depreciate it, or publish books against it. Think you the Lord Jesus Christ would select as administrator of this ordinance a man who before and after administering it in the name of the Holy Trinity would publicly ridicule it as indecent and unbecoming? Does such a man or his work deserve respect? Would any of you be willing to submit to baptism at the hands of a man, or count his baptizing as worthy of recognition, who to gain a member or for any other purpose, will administer a religious rite against his own conscience and then deride his own act? Be sure the law of baptism provides a different sort of administrator. This ordinance was committed to those who loved it and were themselves obedient to it. But more definitely, to whom? Note carefully that the occasion was by special appointment before his death (Matt. 26:32), repeated after his resurrection (Matt. 28:7-10; Mark 16:7), designating a particular mountain in far-off Galilee (Matt. 28:16). From two passages in Matthew (26:32; 28:16) we know the eleven apostles were present, the highest officials in his kingdom.

From others (Matt. 28:7, 10, 17; Mark 16:7; 1 Cor. 15:6) it appears that it was a gathering of the church, including disciples in Galilee as well as from Jerusalem. To these disciples, his *ecclesia,* "the called out," themselves baptized believers and organized, with officers and laws, to them he committed this law of baptism. The apostles themselves, prophets, teachers, healers, pastors, and evangelists were all "set in the church" (1 Cor. 12:28; Eph. 4:11-16). Officers, whether special or ordinary, passed away, but the church was an abiding institution (Matt. 16:18) and to be forever

⇥ Baptism in Water ⇤

"the pillar and ground of the truth" (1 Tim. 3:15); with power to fill offices when vacated by unworthiness or death (Acts 1:15-26; 6:1-6; 2 Tim. 2:2; 1 Tim. 3:1-16; Titus 1:5-9), that the ministry of the word might be perpetuated. So that the law of baptism was committed to his church, to be administered by officers of its own appointment until "the end of the world." Bear this fact in mind: The administrator of baptism ought not only in his individual capacity to be one who loves, honors, and has himself obeyed this ordinance, but particularly he must have been directly appointed thereto by God himself, in originally establishing his kingdom, or ever afterward by the church, Christ's executive on earth till he comes again. An official act must be performed by an officer. An officer must have been put in office by the organization under which he holds office and to which he is responsible for the exercise of official functions.

Take a simple illustration: It has been said that a Welshman recently arrived in this country, and being desirous of citizenship, but ignorant of the method of becoming a citizen, stated his desire to an Irish friend whom he had known in the old country. The Irishman, willing to serve his friend in so laudable a purpose, procured a form of the oath of naturalization, administered it solemnly to the Welshman and gave him a certificate of the fact as evidence thereof. But when the Welshman, at the next election, sought to exercise the privilege of citizenship, he was challenged by one of the judges of the election: "Are you a citizen of this country?" "I am." "Where is the proof of your naturalization?" The Irishman's certificate was submitted and rejected. The Welshman protests: "Why, I am a citizen at heart, and have sincerely taken the prescribed oath in the very words of the law, and honestly intended thereby to comply with the law, and here is written evidence from the good man who administered the oath." To whom the inexorable judge: "My friend, we do not dispute anything you say. Your good intentions and your state of heart are not denied. But the law which prescribed the oath you took also prescribes who shall administer it. No matter how good a man your Irish friend may be, nor how honest his purpose, he had no legal authority to administer the oath to you. Your certificate is no more than blank paper; you must stand aside until you comply with the law."

So baptism is null and void unless administered by legal authority, no matter what the intent or act of the subject or administrator. No organization can stand which leaves to aliens the administration of its laws, and particularly its initiatory ordinances. Let us now consider

II. The subjects of baptism.

Who must be baptized? What says the law? "Go ye, therefore, make disciples of all nations, baptizing them." Is this command of Jesus in harmony with the example of Jesus? Let us appeal to the record: "Jesus made and baptized more disciples than John" (John 4: 1). This is valuable testimony, because:

1. Those to whom the law of baptism is now entrusted were quite familiar with his previous example, which so clearly and authoritatively interprets and construes in advance the law given to them.

2. It shows that Jesus, during his lifetime and in their presence, first made disciples and then baptized them. The very thing they are now required to do.

3. It shows that John the Baptist also, with whose work they were equally familiar, first made disciples and then baptized them.

It follows that as they knew how John made disciples before baptizing them, and how Jesus made disciples before baptizing them, they were instructed by these examples how they were to make disciples before baptizing them. They could not be ignorant of the import of this term of the law, "make disciples," since it had been already construed and its meaning fixed by the Lawgiver himself. Nor need we be

⇥ Baptism in Water ⇤

ignorant, since the record of what John and Jesus did is before us. How, then, did Jesus and John make disciples? Hear the record: "John verily baptized with the baptism of **re**pentance, saying unto the people, that they should believe on him which should come after him, that is, on Christ Jesus" (Acts 19: 4). "Now, after that John was put in prison, Jesus came into Galilee, preaching the gospel of the kingdom of God, and saying, The time is fulfilled, and the kingdom of God is at hand, repent ye, and believe the gospel" (Mark 1:14,15).

These scriptures are very clear. They show that John and Jesus both preached the gospel. That they called on their hearers to do two things—repent and believe. That those who repented of their sins and believed in the Lord Jesus Christ were ready for baptism. In plain words, that repentance and faith constituted discipleship. To make disciples, therefore, means that by preaching the gospel men should be led to repentance and faith. John refused to baptize the impenitent and unbelieving Pharisees, who sought baptism on account of their being natural descendants of Abraham. (See the record, Matt. 3:7-9.) Of Jesus also it is said: "But as many as received him, to them gave he power to become the sons of God, even to them that believe on his name; who were born, not of blood, nor of the will of the flesh, nor of the will of man, but of God" (John 1:12, 13).

It is perfectly clear from the testimony of the four Gospels, that only children of God were to be baptized. Referring to the Spirit's work they must be born from above (John 3:3-8). Referring to the exercises of their own minds, to which they were led by the regenerating Spirit, they repented toward God and believed on Jesus Christ. Two other considerations made it impossible for the disciples to whom Jesus committed the law of baptism to misunderstand its import: First, their own experience. They knew how they were discipled. They knew what had been required of them. Second, to guard them effectually and infallibly from the mistakes of a treacherous memory, the Holy Spirit was promised to them, whose abiding inspiration would bring to their remembrance everything that Jesus had done or taught" (John 14:26; 16: 13).

To put our own minds at rest forever on this subject, we need only one more testimony, which is also here before us. From the subsequent record do we find, as a matter of historical fact, that the church, carrying out this law of baptism, made disciples before baptizing them, and required the same constituent elements of discipleship—repentance and faith? In other words, how did their deeds construe the law? We find an answer in the book of their deeds, called "The Acts of the Apostles." Of the assembled Jews, gathered to the national feasts in Jerusalem out of all nations under heaven, those only who repented and gladly received Peter's word were baptized (Acts 2:38-41).

When Philip preached in Samaria he baptized only men and women who believed the gospel (Acts 8:12). When Peter preached to the Gentiles in Caesarea, they were not baptized until God had granted unto them "repentance unto life," and had "purified their hearts by faith" (Acts 10:47; 11:18; 15:3). The jailer and his household at Philippi were not baptized until all had heard the gospel preached and "rejoiced, believing in God" (Acts 16:30-34).

Only after the Corinthians had heard and believed we're they baptized (Acts 18:8). Indeed, Paul announced the universality and perpetuity of the law to the Ephesian elders at Miletus: "Testifying, both to the Jews and also to the Greeks, repentance toward God and faith toward our Lord Jesus Christ" (Acts 20:21), and be declared to the Hebrews the doctrinal foundation: "Therefore, leaving the principles of the doctrine of Christ, let us go on unto perfection; not laying again the foundation of repentance from dead works and of faith toward God" (Heb. 6:1).

Because the scriptures are so clear, so unequivocal, and so

⇥ Baptism in Water ⇤

numerous, which teach that to make disciples is equivalent to leading men to repentance and faith, I said this morning in the sermon that I would let my right arm drop to my side in everlasting paralysis before I would do so rebellious, so unlawful a thing as to baptize man, woman, or child without evidence of personal discipleship—personal repentance and personal faith. No man living can show any warrant in the New Testament for other subjects of baptism. The best scholars of those who baptize other subjects than penitent believers, admit there is neither plain precept nor example in the New Testament to justify their practice. They might have said that the New Testament is as silent as the grave concerning any other subjects of baptism. And yet baptism is a New Testament ordinance. There alone we find the law which enjoins it. That law admits of no exception for king or peasant, male or female, young or aged. Suppose I should baptize an impenitent unbeliever, who believed neither in the Father, Son, nor Holy Spirit. How would my formula sound: "I baptize thee into the name of the Father, and of the Son, and of the Holy Spirit? "Would it not be more than a farce? Would it not express falsehood?

III. What is the baptism itself.

While I could prove to you from the lexicons and from usage, that the Greek word baptizo means to dip or immerse as much as our English word "dip "means to dip or immerse; and while among unbiased scholars this question is as much settled as the fact that Columbus discovered America or that Cornwallis surrendered at Yorktown; and while if physically able I could cite authority and admissions until the rising sun, I prefer to take the Book itself and show you from inspired words just what baptism is. I will let scripture interpret scripture.

Just here let me impress one thought, which, if carefully considered, will save you from any trouble whatever about Greek lexicons, or citations from the classics: The Lord Jesus Christ himself fixed the meaning of the word forever by his own baptism. Admit for argument's sake that the word had a thousand meanings, in the act of his baptism he designated the particular meaning which would define his ordinance. When John baptized him, no matter how many modes the word might admit, the things which John did, and he did only one thing, settles the mode forever.

Now if I can satisfy myself from the record what John did to Jesus, that ends the controversy for me. I am going to follow him. It matters nothing to me what kings and queens and lords have done. Nor do I care what my father or mother or wife has done. I will follow Jesus; and his disciples, to whom he committed the law to baptize, should understand from his example what meaning he attached to the word. We have before us, therefore, but a short and simple task. Here are all the scriptures which tell of the baptism of Jesus: "Then cometh Jesus from Galilee to Jordan unto John, to be baptized of him. But John forbade him saying, I have need to be baptized of thee, and comest thou to me? And Jesus answering, said unto him, Suffer it to be so now; for thus it becometh us to fulfill all righteousness. Then he suffered him. And Jesus, when he was baptized, went up straightway out of the water; and, lo, the heavens were opened unto him, and he saw the Spirit of God descending like a dove, and lighting on him, and, lo, a voice from heaven, saying, This is my beloved Son in whom I am well pleased "(Matt. 3: 13-17).

"And it came to pass in those days, that Jesus came from Nazareth of Galilee, and was baptized of John in Jordan. And straightway coming up out of the water, he saw the heavens opened, and the Spirit like a dove descending upon him. And there came a voice from heaven, saying, Thou art my beloved Son, in whom I am well pleased "(Mark 1:9-11).

"Now when all the people were baptized, it came to pass, that Jesus also being baptized, and praying, the heaven was opened and the Holy Ghost descended in a bodily shape like a dove upon him, and a voice came from heaven, which said, Thou art my beloved Son; in thee I am well pleased" (Luke

⇥ Baptism in Water ⇤

3:21, 22).

"Know ye not, that so many of us as were baptized into Jesus Christ were baptized into his death? Therefore we are buried with him by baptism into death, that like as Christ was raised up from the dead by the glory of the Father, even so we, also, should walk in newness of life. For if we have been planted together in the likeness of his death, we shall be also in the likeness of his resurrection" (Rom. 6:3-5).

"Buried with him in baptism, wherein, also, ye are risen with him, through the faith of the operation of God, who hath raised him from the dead "(Col. 2:12).

These five are all the passages of Scripture which tell of the baptism of Jesus. Now, with this record before us, we are to determine, not *why* Jesus was baptized, but how ? Our object is to determine what was done in order to fix the meaning of a word. Mark carefully the following points

1. He was baptized in a river. Mark says: "In the Jordan," more correctly, "into the Jordan *"(eis)* ("Mark 1:6, 8, 10).

2. That after baptism he came "up out of the water" *(ek)* (Mark 1:10).

3. That in his baptism he was buried. "We are buried with him by baptism" (Rom. 6:4). "Buried with him in baptism" (Col. 2:12).

4. That in his baptism he was also raised up again. "Wherein, also, ye are risen with him" (Col. 2:12).

5. That this burial and resurrection in water was a likeness of his actual burial and resurrection. "For if we have been planted together (revision, 'united together') in the likeness of his death, we shall be also in the likeness of his resurrection "(Rom. 6:5).

Thus the Scripture interprets itself and defines its own terms. Jesus was buried in baptism. We are buried i n baptism. We therefore are buried with him in baptism. Jesus was raised in baptism. We are raised in baptism. Therefore we are risen with him in baptism. The baptism of Jesus was a likeness of his own burial and resurrection; therefore in our baptism we are united with him (revision) in the likeness of his burial and resurrection. That Jesus was immersed in the river Jordan by John the Baptist is as firmly established as a historical fact by unbiased scholarship of all faiths, as that he was born in Bethlehem of Judea. As to the why, unbiased testimonies diverge. As to the how, the fact, the act, they concur. The how, the fact, the act, is what we now seek. What was done to him that he commanded. While the Jordan flows into the Dead Sea, and while the Bible record remains the meaning of the word is fixed. The burial and resurrection in water are essential to the act of baptism enjoined on us. Whether it be in a river, lake, tank, or baptistery, is immaterial. And you now are to be buried with Christ in baptism, and to be raised with him. Such baptism is current coin with all faiths, because ancient, apostolic, biblical.[4]

As late as 1846, the "Methodist Discipline" asserted that Christ was baptized "in the river of the Jordan," and that "buried in baptism" alludes to water-baptism. But I care little for testimony not in the Book itself. That the disciples to whom Christ committed the law of baptism so understood the meaning of the word will appear sufficiently from a single example recorded: "And he commanded the chariot to stand still; and they went down both into the water, both Philip and the eunuch; and he baptized him. And when they were come up out of the water, the Spirit of the Lord caught away Philip, that the eunuch saw him no more; and he went on his way rejoicing" (Acts 8: 38, 39).

---

[4] John Calvin says: "The very word baptize, however, signifies to immerse; and it is certain that immersion was the practice of the ancient church." "Institutes," Vol. 2, chap. 16, p.491. Indeed, nothing on this earth is more certain. John Wesley and Adam Clarks, commenting on Col. 2:12, refer it to immersion.

Baptism in Water

On this passage, Dr. Carson says: "The man who can read it, and not see immersion in it, must have something in his mind unfavorable to the investigation of truth. As long as I fear God, I cannot, for all the kingdoms of the world, resist the evidence of this single document. Nay, had I no more conscience than Satan himself, I could not as a scholar attempt to expel immersion from this account. All the ingenuity of all the critics in Europe could not silence the evidence of this passage. Amidst the most violent perversion that it can sustain on the rack, it will cry out immersion, immersion."[5] I believe it is also Carson who elsewhere says: "The idiot boy who ran after a wagon all the way from Glasgow to Edinburgh to see if the hind wheel would overtake the forewheel had an errand, though it was only a fool's errand. But if Philip and the eunuch descended from that chariot and both went down into the water after anything else for baptism than immersion, they had less, even, than a fool's errand."

Having thus ascertained the administrator, subject, and act of baptism, we have now to consider

IV. The design of baptism.

The purpose of an institution is measured by its importance. And here I would have you recall how earnestly and tearfully during all this meeting I have tried to keep any ordinance of the church or the church itself from coming between the soul and its Saviour. With all the powers of my mind and heart I have exhorted sinners to come to Jesus for life and salvation, and to refrain from ordinances and church connection until they were saved; that salvation is by blood, not water; that salvation is essential to baptism, and not baptism essential to salvation; that Jesus, not the church, is the Saviour; that the Lord adds to the church the saved. But while solicitous to confine the church and its ordinances in proper bounds, I

---

[5] "On Baptism," p. 128.

underestimate neither the one nor the other. Both are of Divine appointment, and both essential to the ends to which they were appointed.

To me baptism is no matter of indifference. Historic memories forbid. It was in the act of baptism that the Messiah was made known (John 1:33; Luke 3:22). Jesus himself walked over dusty roads from Nazareth to Jordan many miles, to be baptized. However unbecoming the sinful and impure may regard it, he, the immaculate One, said it was becoming: "Thus it becometh us to fulfill all righteousness."

The Holy Trinity, in whose triune name we now baptize, were all present at that baptism in the Jordan—the Father audibly; the Spirit visibly; the Son tangibly. Never while that record remains can any pious heart think of baptism without deep emotion. No soul loyal to God can be displeased with an ordinance during whose administration the Father said: "I am well pleased." The dove-like form of the Holy Spirit endorses it to every mind led by the Spirit. To me it will also ever be sacred because Jesus commanded it. To his own example he adds his precept. That soul cannot love Jesus nor be his friend who disregards his words "If ye love me keep my commandments... Ye are my friends if ye do whatsoever I command you "(John 14:15; 15:14). "Obedience is the essence of the law." It has been, perhaps, extravagantly described as that "principle to which polity owes its stability, life its happiness, faith its acceptance, creation its continuance." Inspiration exclaims "Behold, to obey is better than sacrifice, and to hearken than the fat of rams." To my own converted soul—down through eighteen centuries came the voice of Jesus: "Follow me." And like Paul, I can say: "Whereupon I was not disobedient to the heavenly vision."

Unquestionably a positive institution is a test of love and faith. Unquestionably whenever a penitent believer is baptized he "justifies God, and the man who remains impenitent, unbelieving, and unbaptized "rejects the counsel of God against himself" (Luke 7:29, 30).

⇥ Baptism in Water ⇤

Unquestionably a good conscience, purged by the blood (Heb. 9:14) of Christ and proceeding from "a faith unfeigned" (1 Tim. 1:5), and enlightened as to duty, demands baptism as its "answer" (1 Peter 3:21).

But none of these express the design of baptism—the end or purpose for which it was appointed. Close attention to the great facts of the gospel will assist us in understanding its ceremonial ordinances which publicly and visibly declare our hearty acceptance of those facts. The facts are three-fold:

1. God, the Father, so loved the world that he gave his only begotten Son, that whosoever believeth in him, should not perish, but have everlasting life (John 3:16).

2. God, the Son, thus sent of the Father,

(a) died for our sins (1 Cor. 15:1-3);

(b) was buried (1 Cor. 15:4);

(c) was raised again for our justification (1 Cor. 15:4; Acts 2:24; Rom. 4:25);

(d) was made both Lord and Christ (Acts 2:36; Phil. 2:6-11; Heb. 1: 2-12).

3. God, the Holy Ghost, accredits the Son (Matt. 3:16; John 16:13, 14), gives power to his disciples (Acts 1:8), convinces the world of sin, righteousness, and judgment (John 16:7-11).

In these great facts the gospel sets forth Jesus to us—as the Sent of the Father, and the Anointed of the Holy Spirit, O be our Prophet, Priest, and King. Hence when we, in our hearts, receive him thus offered, we are required to publicly and visibly avow our faith. This leads up naturally to the design of baptism.

1. Our baptism is a profession or declaration, public and visible, of our faith in Jesus, as the Sent of the Father and the Anointed of the Spirit, to be our Prophet, Priest,

and King. Hence the prescribed formula: "Baptizing them into the name of the Father, and of the Son, and of the Holy Ghost" (Matt. 28:19). As has been shown, Father, Son, and Holy Spirit were all present, and their respective offices suggestively indicated at the baptism in Jordan (Matt. 3:16, 17). From all which it is conclusive, that baptism must be the personal, individual, and voluntary act of one who Las heart and believed the gospel, otherwise there is nothing to profess or declare. And as we should speedily and candidly profess what we honestly and heartily believe, we are not surprised to find baptism so closely associated in time with the faith which it professes. In apostolic days there was nothing like the modern interval between them. Baptism was at the threshold of religious life. It preceded every other obligation enjoined on the converted. The candle being lighted it was put on the candlestick. We can thus understand why some called it the "initiatory" ordinance, and others "the door" into the church, so interpreting 1 Cor. 12:13: "For by (in) one Spirit are we all baptized into one body; whether we be Jews or Gentiles; whether we be bond or free." If Jesus in the prophetic Psalm (40:10) could say: "I have not hid thy righteousness within my heart; I have declared thy faithfulness and thy salvation: I have not concealed thy lovingkindness and thy truth from the great congregation," so we should not tarry, but hasten to declare in baptism our faith in him who hath saved us.

2. But it is much more than a mere profession or declaration of faith. It publicly expresses and avows our absolute subjection to Jesus Christ as our Teacher, Leader, and Sovereign. It is our voluntary and deliberate pledge, in the sight of heaven, earth, and hell, to accept his teachings as the law of our lives; to obey all his orders without questioning or murmuring; to submit to his government in all things. By baptism into his name we solemnly promise to refer all our perplexities and

differences to him as our infallible oracle, and to accept his decision as supreme and final. If the disciples of Pythagoras, a faulty and fallible philosopher, ended all controversy on a disputed point by saying: "He said it; and he was Pythagoras," how much more should a Christian bow submissively to every *ipse dixit* of our immaculate and infallible Teacher? Baptism is our oath of allegiance to his government. It is our enlistment in his military service and the putting on of the uniform which marks us as soldiers of the Great Captain of our salvation. All of this is expressed by being baptized, not "in," but "into" his name. You will observe that when I baptize you directly, I will say "I baptize you into the name."

When the Jewish fathers were baptized into Moses, though a figurative baptism, it pledged them to him as leader, teacher, and ruler (1 Cor. 10:1-11), disobedience of whose commandments was high treason, and both civil and military insubordination. Because the Corinthians were not baptized into the name of Paul or Cephas or Apollos, these could not be leaders of factions or *nuclei of parties*. Being baptized into Christ, he alone was Leader (1 Cor. 1:12-15; 3:3-6). Hence Paul says: "For as many of you as have been baptized into Christ have put on Christ" (Gal. 3:27). That is, as you lay aside the wet clothing in which you have been baptized and put on dry and fresh apparel, so you have, figuratively, put on Christ as a uniform, marking you and pledging you to his service. If, then, there be deep significance and solemnity in an oath of allegiance to an earthly government in the enlistment and uniform *of* military service, how much more solemn and significant is our baptism into the name of Jesus!

With great emphasis of heart have I endeavored to impress on your minds, at the outset, this part of the design of baptism, because there is generally so little teaching on it, and because so many enter baptism lightly and hold its obligations slightly. To the disobedient, the unruly, the worldlyminded, the quarrelsome, the factious, the backsudden Christian, the question, "Were you not baptized?" ought to be as "the look of the Lord" on Peter, which caused him "to go out and weep bitterly" (Luke 22:61, 62). While expressing all this, our Lord appointed such an ordinance as would at the same time serve another design. Hence

3. Baptism symbolizes our purification or release from sin. Hence Peter, in his great pentecostal sermon says: "Repent ye, and be baptized, every one of you, in the name of Jesus Christ unto the remission *of* your sins" (Acts 2:38, R.V.) Also Paul writes to the Hebrews: "This is the covenant that I will make with them after those days, saith the Lord; I will put my laws on their heart, and upon their minds also will I write them; *then saith he,* And their sins and their iniquities will I remember no more. Now, where remission of these is, there is no more offering for sin. Having therefore, brethren, boldness to enter into the holy place by the blood of Jesus, by the way which he dedicated for us, a new and living way, through the veil, that is to say his flesh; and *having* a great priest over the house of God; let us draw near with a true heart in fullness of faith, having our hearts sprinkled from an evil conscience, and our bodies washed with pure water" (10:16-22, R.V.). On this last scripture Dr. Kendrick, in his commentary, says: "The purifying rites of the old covenant were partly with blood and partly with water. Expiation was symbolized by blood—simply cleansing and moral purity by water. The new covenant meets the old at every point. For the sprinkling of the blood of beasts upon the body it has the sprinkling of the blood of Christ upon the heart. For the lustrations with water, by which the priests cleansed themselves when entering on their duties, and especially for that complete bathing of the body which the high priest underwent before entering the inner sanctuary (Lev. 16:4), the Christian priesthood, every Christian being a priest (1 Peter 2:5; Rev. 1:6), before following Christ within the veil into the presence

of God, must also submit to, the same symbolical cleansing, though vastly more significant. This is clearly baptism— "not the putting away of the filth of the flesh, but the answer of a good conscience toward God." Thus the author unites the outward and the inward; the efficient and the sacramental elements of the Christian life; deliverance from the guilt and power of sin wrought by the Holy Spirit on the application of the blood of Christ to the soul, and then this moral renovation and purity, a death to sin and a resurrection to holiness, symbolized in the bath of baptism."

Any one familiar with the New Testament will readily recall striking expressions about its two simple ordinances, such as: "Jesus took bread and blessed it, and brake it, and gave it to the disciples, and said: "Take, eat; this is my body. And he took the cup, and gave thanks, and gave it to them, saying: Drink ye all of it; for this is my blood of the new testament, which is shed for many for the remission of sins" *eis aphesin amartion* (Matt. 26:28). And: "Be baptized every one of you, for the remission of sins" *eis aphesin amartion* (Acts 2:38). In both these memorial ordinances the language which expresses the end or purpose of them is exactly the same in both the Greek and English, "for the remission of sins." Shutting their eyes to the great heart-fact of the New Testament—that it is the blood of Christ which really cleanses us from all sin (1 John 1:7), and that the ordinances only symbolize this fact—ritualists in all ages have used such expressions as the foregoing citations from Matthew and Acts as the basis of a monstrous system of sacramental salvation. They have enslaved the world to their superstitious blasphemies of transubstantiation, consubstantiation, and baptismal regeneration. To the wafer they have said: "My God," and to the water, "My Saviour." But to you, my brethren, I need not say that you found salvation before you came to the water, and being already justified by faith in the blood of Christ, you will not look into this waiting pool to find remission of your sins. But here you do symbolize that fact in a suitable and striking emblem. Indeed, if any one of you shall even now say that you are not forgiven—if your conscience, purified by the blood of Christ, does not witness in your heartfelt experience that you are now forgiven and saved—I will not baptize you. Where there is no substance let there be no shadow. And as the ordinance which declares your faith iii Christ and your absolute submission to him as Leader, is of such nature that it fitly symbolizes the remission of your sins by that great fact of the gospel, the death of Christ, so it is appointed also as a pictorial representation of other great facts of the gospel. Hence our next point

4. Baptism is a figure or likeness in which we are buried and risen with Christ. Hence it is a monument or memorial of his resurrection, and a pledge and prophecy of our own.

Here let me impress indelibly, and as it were, in letters of fire upon your grateful and newly converted hearts the holy words of inspiration which establish this great design of baptism. I read from the Revised text. "What shall we say then? Shall we continue in sin that grace may abound? God forbid. We who died to sin, how shall we any longer live therein? Or, are ye ignorant that all we who were baptized into Christ Jesus were baptized into his death? We were buried, therefore, with him through baptism into death that like as Christ was raised from the dead through the glory of the Father, so we also might walk in newness of life. For if we have become united with him by the likeness of his death, we shat I be also by the likeness of his resurrection" (Rom. 6:1-5). "In whom (Christ) ye were also circumcised with a circumcision not made with hands, in the putting off of the body of the flesh, in the circumcision of Christ; having been buried with him in baptism, wherein ye were also raised with him through faith in the working of God, who raised him from the dead" (Col. 2:11, 12). "Else what shall they—which are baptized for the dead? If the dead are not raised at all, why then are they baptized for them?" (1 Cor. 15:29). "God

↣ Baptism in Water ↤

waited in the days of Noah, while the ark was a preparing, wherein few, that is eight souls, were saved through water: which also after a true likeness doth now save you, even baptism, not the putting away of the filth of the flesh, but the interrogation of a good conscience toward God, through the resurrection of Jesus Christ" (1 Peter 3:20, 21).

From these several passages certain facts are obvious. Baptism, being a burial, implies a previous death. This was a death to sin and the world. This death was effected by the Holy Spirit in regeneration. This regeneration or "circumcision of the heart, circumcision not made with hands," was prefigured by the circumcision of the flesh—the circumcision made with hands. (See also the following scriptures: Rom. 2:28, 29; Gal. 5:6; 6:12; Phil. 3:3.) Hence, regeneration and not baptism came in the place of circumcision; that being dead to sin by regeneration, the Christian should he buried; that this burial is baptism; that this water-burial of the Christian is a likeness of Christ's burial in the ground. Hence, it is a monument of that fact. That this water-resurrection is a likeness of Christ's resurrection from the grave, and is therefore a monument of that fact. Hence, baptism saves us, not really, but in this likeness, being the likeness of Christ's resurrection. That it is also a pledge and prophecy of our own resurrection, and is so used by Paul in his great argument on the resurrection. That implying a previous death to sin, and representing a resurrection to a new life, it obligates us to walk in newness of life.

And now, brethren, you can understand and appreciate my great affection for this ordinance—why I would not have it changed; why I desire it to remain on the earth while death and sorrow reign. I stand in the graveyard to plead for its integrity and perpetuity. All around me they are sleeping — your dead and mine. There is father's grave; and here by him mother sleeps; and that little rounded hillock covers my baby. Ah! the pain when he left me. That clod hit my heart which rudely fell on the coffin lid under which little waxen fingers were folded on a pulseless breast. Oh, the dead! the dead, who have left us! Is there no sign that they will live again? Yes, while water flows, while it stands in pools, while in placid lakes it mirrors the downlooking stars, while oceans surround land, there will be a voice—the voice of mighty waters. It is the voice of the swollen tides of the Mississippi, and Amazon, and Orinoco, and the Nile, and the De la Plats, and the Danube, and the Rhine. The echo of the surf of the great lakes and inland seas. Yea, it is the storm-roar of the Arctic, Antarctic, Indian, Pacific, and Atlantic Oceans, this voice of many waters carried down by every river, the echoes of its baptisms, down to the shoreless seas and by them caught up in storm trumpets loud enough to sound beyond the stars and announce to the disembodied spirits of the just made perfect: THERE WILL BE A RESSURECTION OF THE DEAD.

More than once since I have been pastor here I have gone from a baptism in yonder Brazos in unchanged clothes, to stand by the graves of my dead in yonder cemetery and say "Little ones, you will not sleep forever. The resurrection is coming. I have just seen its monument and heard its prophecy." What if a foreign vandal should begin to tear down Bunker Hill monument? What would Boston, Massachusetts, the nation say? "No; never. Let it stand."

> There let it stand until the river
>   That flows beneath shall cease to flow.
> Aye, until that hill itself shall quiver
>   With nature's last expiring throe.

That monument perpetuates the memory of a nation's birth. And so when any one would lay sacrilegious hand on this monument, which perpetuates the victory over death and the redemption of a world, I would say: "No. For the sake of the dead, no. Because of the sad-hearted and griefstricken who mourn for them, no. Let not superstition mar it, nor impiety raze it. It forecasts the resurrection. It prophesies that death will die."

Baptism in Water

Here my sermon ought to end. But a stumbling-block needs removal. Some tender consciences, thoroughly satisfied about baptism, have been troubled about communion. Unable to gainsay the testimony of God's word as to the administrator, subject, act, and design of baptism, a whisper about "close communion "has sought to sidetrack them into disobedience. The whisper was forked: (1.) "No relation of order between baptism and communion." (2.) "Baptized there you never can show Christian fellowship by communing with your friends and kindred of other denominations. Elsewhere things are broader." Now, if you attended to the first part of this sermon you saw a divinely appointed relation of order between baptism and communion. (1.) Disciple. (2.) Baptize the disciples. (3.) Teach the baptized disciples to observe all other commandments. This order is so plainly taught in the Bible that until quite modern times no one questioned it. History mentions no violation of this order for more than sixteen hundred years after the death of Christ. It was not so *very* long ago a distinguished divine of another denomination said: "No church ever gave the communion to any persons before they were baptized. Among all the absurdities that ever were held, none ever maintained that any person should partake of the communion before they were baptized."[6]

The scholars as a class, and the denominations as a rule, concur in the statement. A few open-communion Baptists and some sections of two other denominations are the exceptions. In our aspirations after "broadness" we should be careful to be no broader than the law, and when we are "liberal "let it be with our own things, and not the things of another. The ordinances are God's, not ours. Satan preached broadness to Eve with direful results.

"In one spirit are we all baptized into one body." And what is the body? The church. And what is the Lord's Supper? An ordinance in the church, never outside.

---

[6] Dr. Wall, "History Infant Baptism," part 2, chapter 9.

What says another distinguished divine, not of our denomination: "It is an indispensable qualification for this ordinance that the candidate for communion be a member of the visible church of Christ, in full standing. By this I intend that he should be a person of piety; that he should have made a public profession of religion, and that he should have been baptized."[7]

Dr. Hibbard, the great Northern Methodist author, expressly endorses the Baptist position on communion. For myself, I would rather die than administer the Lord's Supper to any one, as an individual, in his room, whether he be well or sick. It may never be observed except by a local church gathered together in one place. Baptism precedes the supper. So Christ ordained. I have no purpose or desire to question his wisdom or to be "liberal and broad "at his expense. In religion we should be scrupulous to do nothing in God's name except upon God's orders. Give us precepts and examples from his word. I do not care a jot for a man's word in matters of religion. Nor would I abate a jot of God's word to gain a thousand members.

Now to the other fork of the whisper: When you partake of the Lord's Supper, what is your purpose? Why do you commune? I press you for an answer? And I want a Bible answer. Jesus said: "Do this in remembrance of me." It memorializes his death. It is not to show your fellowship for some other Christian, nor for a friend, nor for a kinsman, nor for wife or husband, parent or child, brother or sister. Scourged from our hearts be every image but the marred face of Jesus when we partake of his supper. Let that face fill our vision. Show as much Christian fellowship or love for kindred and friends as you please, but do not prostitute the Lord's Supper from its high purpose to such ends.

Every day of my life I delight to show Christian fellowship to any disciple of Jesus. If he has repented of his sins and

---

[7] Dwight's "System," Theological Sermon, 160.

Baptism in Water

heartily received Jesus Christ as a Saviour, he is my brother, whether he be Jew or Gentile, bond or free. I don't care what name he goes by, I love him. But I will not partake of the Lord's Supper to show my fellowship for him. Much as I love him, I do not exalt him in my Redeemer's place. Participation in the supper for such purposes is sin and high treason. Let the monuments stand as Christ ordained them and where he placed them.

And now, dear brethren and sisters, the hour has come for you to be baptized. As you have gladly received his word, I would have you joyfully obey this command. I never shall forget the day I was baptized. Oh, dear friends, if you could ever know (God grant you may never know it experimentally) the horrors of hell through which I passed in my infidelity, then you might know the joy of my conversion, when I saw my Redeemer, when I fell at his feet and said in my heart: "Lord, tell me what to do, I'll do it without a question." So when I took his Book and read about baptism I went to the church and asked to make a statement. They gathered around me to hear. I told my experience and asked to be baptized. Lovingly they received me and we went down to old Davidson Creek, in Burleson County, and there an old schoolmate, W.W. Harris, called the Spurgeon of Texas, baptized me. As I went down into the water I thought of Christ's burial and my own future burial. I saw myself cold in death. I thought of Christ's triumphant resurrection. I felt in mind the earthquake shock and heard the chains of the terrible one bound to his chariot. The supernal glory of his demonstrated divinity illumined my heart. I thought of my own future resurrection, the trumpet sound, the waking dead, the white throne of judgment, and my place at his right hand; my heart overflowed with love and joy and peace. I can see it all now; time does not dim the picture. So I would have you to be baptized.

A Discussion of the Lord's Supper

A DISCUSSION OF THE LORD'S SUPPER.[1]

(This sermon is respectfully and kindly dedicated to all fair-minded, truth-loving Pedo-Baptists. Most earnestly does the author disclaim any intention or desire to wound their feelings, but makes his appeal to their reason and love of justice.—*B.H. CARROLL,* Pastor, First Baptist Church, Waco, Texas.)

TEXT: *Be ye followers of me even as I also am of Christ. Now I praise you, brethren, that ye * * * kept the ordinances as I delivered them to you * * * For I have received of the Lord, that which I also delivered unto you, etc.*—I COR. 11:1, 2, 23.

OR preaching this sermon, my own mind is satisfied with the following reasons:

1. It is ever the duty of the pastor to instruct his congregation in doctrine. Especially is this so with regard to positive institutions. Everything relating to a positive institution should be clearly set forth and understood. What is it, and how is it to be administered?

2. The scriptural observance of the Lord's Supper is inseparably connected with efficient church discipline.

3. Several true, earnest Christians, who are anxious to do right, and therefore seek to know the truth, have requested me to preach on this subject. They are Baptists

---

[1] Carroll, B. H. *Christ and His Church.* Ed., J. B. Cranfill. Nashville: Broadman Press, 1940. 135-168.

upon all other points. Upon this, their minds have been perplexed and annoyed by suggestions from without and doubt from within. This sermon is for them.

4. I am desirous of relieving my beloved church from unjust censure—from the unwarrantable charges of bigotry and illiberality.

5. Restricted communion is necessary not only to the well-being but to the perpetuity of Baptist churches.

6. Its importance to the prosperity and perpetuity of Baptist churches, makes it the chief point of attack by our enemies. They evidently regard it as our Gibraltar. Beyond all question it is the citadel of our beloved Zion—that key position, which when once lost, ultimately necessitates the lowering of our flag all along the line of our fortifications. When then the enemy makes any one of our distinctive features the chief point of attack, let that assailed principle be our chief point of defense. In defense let me not be content with exculpating our close communion from the charge of bigotry, but make a sally beyond our fortifications and establish in the sight of God's truth THE SIN OF OPEN COMMUNION.

7. As the last reason necessary now to assign, it is claimed that this attack is masked. It is not an outright, downright assault. It appears to be masked because

(a) *Communion with the Baptists is evidently not the thing desired.* A careful survey of the situation would not lead us to conclude that their solicitude for inter-communion is the occasion of all the mighty outbreaks of indignation against "close communion."

(b) I regard the attack as masked because they make no war on the principles which underlie the communion question. All denominations, with remarkable unanimity, agree to the principles which control the communion. If they admit that the tree is good, let there be no quarrel with

A Discussion of the Lord's Supper

the fruit.

(c) The attack seems masked because it is generally made in private circles, where it cannot be met. The mischief is accomplished before it is discovered. "I like Baptists very much. I have charity for all denominations, but Oh! *that close communion!*"

(d) Yet again it seems masked, because sophistries are used instead of arguments. That is, they use a word that has a different meaning in the conclusion from what it has in the premise. It is adroitly managed by a misuse of terms to array against our communion of bread and wine the scriptural communion of heaven and the Christian communion of earth.

(e) It is masked because the true Baptist position is misstated. What Baptist minister accustomed to conduct his protracted meetings has not met with these difficulties? How often he leaves a young convert, happy in the hope of glory and about ready to obey the Savior, to find on his next visit that something has intervened. The convert hesitates, speaks evasively and ambiguously. What is the difficulty? It seems to have no head, no shape, no tangible form. Perhaps at last it will be developed that somebody has made an impression on the young convert's mind that Baptists "will get people to work for them and they won't feed them;" that "they believe baptism essential to salvation;" that "they unchristianize other denominations;" that "they refuse to receive people that the Lord Jesus Christ receives;" that "in heaven they are going to have a separate table from the rest of the redeemed;" that "they separate the husband and the wife from the same communion table, though the Lord has said, 'What God has joined together, let not man put asunder.'" In a word, that "they are exclusive, illiberal and bigoted."

These are some of the reasons that have induced me to discuss this subject today. The discussion is entered in kindness, bluntness and with such ability as I possess. Preparatory to the discussion, let terms be defined.

What is communion?

Joint participation of the Lord's Supper.

What is Free or Open Communion?

That in which everybody, *without any restrictions whatever, is* invited and allowed to partake.

Without the fear of successful contradiction, I affirm that there is *none such in the world.* Upon a real *bonaa fide* open communion table the sun of God or the light of stars or lamp or torch never shone.

What is Close, or Restricted Communion?

When a church administering the ordinance limits the invitation to participate. ALL IN THE WORLD ARE SUCH. Some have fewer limitations than others but all have limitations. Some open the door wider than others, but all open it.

With regard to restrictions, they are either HUMAN OR DIVINE. The divine are to be observed, the human rejected. It is the acknowledged prerogative of the Son of God "to open so that no man can shut, and to shut so that no man can open." In all the universe lives there no intelligence high enough in authority to lift from the communion table of Jehovah a single restriction imposed by Almighty God.

From what ought communion to be free?

Dare the arch angel affirm that it is free from a Divine limitation? Who of the created beings presumes to impose a limit more than Jehovah has imposed? It is a remarkable fact, attested by the Word of God, that the prevalence of a human restriction or tradition *makes void* the Divine.

A Discussion of the Lord's Supper

God has said, "Thou shalt honor thy father and thy mother."

The Pharisee by his limitation of that commandment made void the law of God by his tradition. (See Mark 7:11.) Let this fact and illustration be retained in mind for application after a while.

In this connection it is proper to call attention to the obstinacy of error—to mark its power of retention and tenacity of life. It may be embedded in truth, like a worm in the heart of an apple. It may be as tares in a wheat field, planted when the ground was made mellow for the reception of the good seed. As the tares have grown up side by side with the wheat, so has error matured side by side with truth. To pull it up seems to uproot truth. It may be a false thread interwoven in the warp and woof of a fabric of cloth. To destroy it you must rend the garment. It may have been made sacred by hallowed associations. To assail it seems to lift a hand of sacrilege against holy things.

Like the devil, it comes as an angel of light. It may be so connected with marriage that to smite it seems to strike that holy institution of God. It may be so associated with maternity that he who assails it is regarded as the murderer of a mother's joys, as one who mocks her sorrows. It may be so associated with old age—with burials—with the holidays of a people, that to strike it seems like scorning the hoary head—like overturning the tombstones of the dead—like calling of a weary people from their festivities.

When a man has thus imbibed error, to abandon it seems to repudiate his childhood, to abjure parental influence, to pull off the wedding ring, to tear down the Christmas garlands and to strip life of its sweetest memories. Every passion, every prejudice of his nature is aroused. His ear cannot hear the truth, his eye cannot see its beauty, his heart cannot receive it. A direct attack upon the error is as mad as the charge of the "Light Brigade." He who assaults it is regarded as a personal enemy. No power of argument, no array of facts, no accumulation of testimony, though "Pelion be on Ossa piled," can move him.

The only remedy is to let the error alone. Fight it not. But teach truth. Truth received into the heart expels the error. *The expulsive power of truth received is the only hope.* They must be led to consider religion as relating to God, that repentance is towards God, faith is in God, that Jesus and His authority are higher than father, mother, brother, sister, husband or wife.

One of the most seductive and at the same time fatal forms of error is a FALSE LIBERALITY, a spurious charity, a fictitious sentimentality. Instead of "rejoicing in the truth," it rejoices in uniting with everybody, in admitting all claims, in fellowshipping all claimants. He who opposes this broad platform of never-ending compromise is ostracized as a bigot.

With this statement of these preliminaries the question is now asked, WHAT IS THE BAPTIST POSITION?

"It is an indispensable qualification for this ordinance, that the candidate for communion be a member of the church of Christ in full standing; that he shall be a person of piety; that he should have made a public profession of religion; and that he should have been baptized."

I suppose there is not a close communion Baptist on earth who would refuse to receive this as expressive of his position. To a man they would endorse it, item by item, and as a whole. And yet this is the language of Timothy Dwight, D. D., President of Yale College, and Professor of Divinity in that institution—the Agamemnon of Pedo-Baptists. What then, according to this great Presbyterian, are the qualifications for communion?

1. Church membership.

2. Good standing in the church, that is, he must not be under discipline. The idea is that communion and church discipline are co-extensive.

A Discussion of the Lord's Supper

And what are his qualifications for church membership?

1. Practical piety.

2. Profession of religion.

3. Baptism.

Where is there a Baptist who wants communion any closer than that? That such a platform is derived from the Word of God, let us see what are the doctrines of the text.

1. Jesus delivered His ordinance to Paul (I Cor. 11:23). God alone is lawgiver. He ordains—churches keep ordinances.

2. Just what Paul received he delivered to the church. See I Cor. 1:1 and the text.

3. Just what they received they were to keep, maintain, perpetuate.

4. They were to keep the ordinances as he *delivered* them, in the place, in the manner and for the object instituted.

5. Paul himself, though he had been caught up to the third heaven, was to be followed only, as he followed Christ. Mark the power of this last doctrine. Paul elsewhere said, "Though an angel from heaven teach any other gospel, let him be accursed." Gal. 1:8.

"Teaching them to observe all things whatsoever I have commanded you," were among the last words of Jesus. Matt. 28:20. "Let God be true but every man be a liar." Rom. 3:4. "All flesh is as grass, and all the glory of man as the flower of grass. The grass withereth and the flower thereof fadeth away; *but the word of the Lord endureth forever.*" I Peter 1:24.

If there be any force in this doctrine, corroborated by these Scriptures, why is it that some hesitate to obey truth because so many wise, good men preach and practice error?

6. The sixth doctrine of the text is that the church received praise, in faithfully observing God's commandments. I Cor. 11:1, 2.

7. That the church was condemned in making any departure from the divine requirement. I Cor. 11:22.

As an illustration of the last two doctrines, take the decree referred to in Acts 15:28. This decree was referred to the churches to be kept. Acts. 16:4. For failing to keep it the Savior threatened to remove the candlestick of one of the seven churches of Asia. Rev. 2:14.

With these seven doctrines of the text confronting us, let us ask the following questions:

Was the church of Corinth free to substitute the paschal lamb for the appointed bread and wine? Were they free to add bitter herbs to the elements of communion? Were they free to withhold the cup from the laity, when the Savior had said, *"All* ye drink of it?" Were they free to set the table *out of the kingdom,* when the Savior had said, "I appoint unto a kingdom—to eat and to drink at my table *in my kingdom?"* Luke 22:30. Were they free to commune to *satisfy hunger and thirst,* when Paul said, "What! have ye not houses to eat and to drink in? or despise ye the church of God?" I Cor. 17:22. Was "the believing wife" (I Cor. 7:13) allowed to commune with her unbelieving husband, when the Word declares, "Ye cannot drink the cup of the Lord and the cup of devils; ye cannot be partakers of the Lord's table and the table of devils?" Were they free to commune as individuals or in groups, when Paul said, "My brethren, when ye come together to eat, tarry one for another?" I Cor. 11:33. Were they free to extend the communion to a man not in good standing, when God's Word emphatically commands, "But now I have written unto you not to keep company, if any man that is called a brother be a fornicator, or covetous, or idolater, or a railer, or a drunkard, or an extortioner, *with such a one no not to eat?"*

A Discussion of the Lord's Supper

Has any church on earth the right to tempt a man "to eat and drink damnation to himself?" And yet the Word of God declared that every communicant does this who "does not discern the Lord's body." I Cor. 11:29. And as spiritual things have to be "spiritually discerned," (I Cor. 2:14), which is by faith, were they free to invite a man to commune who had no saving faith in Christ?

A heretic after the first and second admonition was to be rejected (Titus 3:10), and they were commanded to withdraw from the disorderly, II Thess. 3:6. A man thus rejected, from whom the fellowship of the church was withdrawn, was to be to them as "a heathen man and a publican," Matt. 18:17.

Now, were they to have a communion so *open* that this excluded heretic could come up to the communion table of that church from which he had been expelled? Any right thinking mind, attentively considering the bearing of these questions, must conclude that Almighty God is the author of close communion.

Having read the Baptist position in the language of President Dwight, I now submit it in the language of a Baptist, with some of the terms defined:

"We believe the Scriptures teach that CHRISTIAN BAPTISM is the immersion in water, of a believer, by a qualified administrator, to show forth in a solemn and beautiful emblem our faith in the crucified, buried and risen Savior, with its effect in our death to sin, burial from the world and resurrection to newness of life; that this baptism is a prerequisite to the privileges of a church relation, among which is the Lord's Supper, in which the members of the church, by the sacred use of bread and wine are to commemorate together the dying love of Christ; always preceded by solemn, self-examination."

With this position before us, let us test some of the objections urged against our practice.

B.H. Carroll

Query 1st. Is the Baptist practice censurable because it is the "Lord's table"?

Surely they cannot be censured because they fail to teach that it is the Lord's table. With great emphasis they quote Jesus as saying, "My table," Luke 22:30. And Paul, in calling it "the Lord's table," and "the cup of the Lord," I Cor. 10:21.

John, the first Baptist, never denied more emphatically that he was the Christ than Baptists since then have disclaimed all ownership in the Lord's table. With remarkable unanimity they say, "To our own private table we cordially invite Pedo-Baptists, but God alone can invite to His table."

It is equally evident that they cannot be justly censured in declaring *what is meant by* its being the Lord's table. They say it is His table because—

1. He instituted it, I Cor. 11:23-25; Matt. 26:26.

2. He prescribed the elements, bread and wine.

3. He located it "In His kingdom," in His church, (Luke 22:29), and compare I Cor. 1:1 with I Cor. 11:22, 23.

4. He distinctly stated its object: "This do in remembrance of me—as oft as ye do this ye do show my death until I come."

5. He defined qualifications for the communicant, that he must be a disciple, a penitent believer, a baptized man. Not only baptized, but a member of the church and in good standing. Less than this no church of Jesus can require. This, according to Dr. Dwight, is God's law of communion.

6. It is the Lord's table, because He fixes even the manner of observing it. Communicants must eat and drink in a worthy manner. That decorum and solemnity becoming the church of God in remembering earth's greatest tragedy must be observed. It was no heathen festival—no

A Discussion of the Lord's Supper

drunken orgy of Bacchus.

7. As the Lord's table, and not a table of the church, Jehovah left no arbitrary discretion to the church, as to the bidding of guests, but fixed, by express and irrevocable statutes, the character of the communicant. As the church was to withhold the bread and wine from the heretic, the heathen, the adulterer, the covetous man and all that walked disorderly, the Lord of the Table, by this prohibition, made the CHURCH and not the INDIVIDUAL the judge of heresy, adultery, covetousness and order.

8. It is the Lord's table, because He alone must prescribe in what the *communicant must judge.* The judge cannot read the heart. In communion the Lord's body and blood must be discerned—spiritually discerned. Our faith must see Him and rest in Him. Without this faith we eat and drink condemnation to ourselves, though we be members of the church. Nor is the church to blame if we have made credible profession of religion and in all outward deportment carried ourselves circumspectly and prudently. A tree may be covered with green foliage and yet be rotten to the core on the inside. Their heart may be as empty of life as a blasted nut. This is a matter between the communicant and the heart-searching God. Hence, to every church member the law is, "Let a man *examine himself,* and so let him eat."

These then are some of the considerations that induce Baptists to believe, teach and call it the Lord's table. They mean by it that Jesus instituted it, located it, prescribed the elements, object of it, qualifications of communicants, manner of observing it, in what the churches were to judge and in what the individual communicant. Can any reasonable censure be attached to their construction of the phrase, "the Lord's table"?

But perhaps they censure us because of the conclusions we

deduce from this construction. With Christian candor and fairness, let us examine their deduction, and see if bigotry does not lurk in it.

The Baptist Conclusion.—As it is not our table, but the Lord's, it is unhallowed presumption and rebellion for a church to violate any of these requirements of the Master. We dare not add one. Noah, however indignant at the blasphemies of the people before the flood, dared not shut the door of the ark as long as God's Spirit was striving. And after God shut the door, he dared not take in any drowning wretch through the window. While this is not in itself a question of salvation, it is a question of obedience to God.

Over our own table we have authority. We can set it where we please in the parlor, dining room or yard. We can put on it what viands we please, invite whom we please, and withhold invitation from any. God has left some things to our control. As a beautiful and forcible illustration of the distinction between the personal right of the subject and the right of the sovereign, I quote from Sir Walter Scott. King James of Scotland had sent the English Ambassador, Lord Marmion, to be entertained by the Earl of Douglas. When about to leave the castle of Douglas, Lord Marmion said, holding out his hand:

> "Part we in friendship from your land,
>   And, noble Earl, receive my hand."
> But Douglas round him drew his cloak,
>   Folded his arms, and thus he spoke: —
> "My manors, halls and bowers shall still
>   Be open at my sovereign's will,
> To each one whom he lists, howe'er
>   Unmeet to be the owners here;
> My castles are my king's alone
>   From turret to foundation stone, —
> The hand of Douglas is his own,
>   And never shall in friendly grasp
> The hand of such as Marmion clasp."

A Discussion of the Lord's Supper

But it is charged against us that we get others "to work for us and then will not feed them—that we will not eat with other Christians—that we deny hospitality and Christian courtesies to Pedo-Baptists." These are grave charges and ought not to be lightly made. Is it true that Baptists are dishonest, denying food to the laborer? Do they go beyond the Pharisees, who would not eat with publicans and sinners, and actually decline to sit down at the same private board with other Christians? Are they so inhospitable as to shut their doors in the face of Pedo-Baptist guests? *In the name of Almighty God I deny it,* and call for proof of that which, without proof, is slander.

"Oh, no!" they say, "you misunderstand us; we are not talking about your house, your table; but you will not invite us to the Lord's table." Then in the name of fairness, why use equivocal expressions? Why array prejudices against us by casting a reflection upon our courtesy, hospitality and honesty? The world knows that Baptists are behind no denomination in welcoming guests to their homes, tables and hearthstones.

Brethren, Baptist brethren, set *your* table where you will, but dare not move the *Lord's table* out of the church. Invite at your discretion to your own board, *but allow the same privilege to Almighty God.* Usurp not the prerogative of Jevovah. If a man is hungry, feed him from your own table, but appease not his hunger with the sacramental bread. Do not rob God that you may appear benevolent. Upon all proper occasions show your fellowship for all Christians, and your regard for the sacred relations of husband and wife. But don't prostitute the Lord's Supper for such a purpose. Lead the poor sinner to the Savior, but dare not administer God's holy ordinance to him as a "means of grace." God never intended to make baptism and the Lord's Supper converting agencies.

Shall we quail before the loud clamor raised against us? Shall unjust charges of bigotry and inhospitality coerce us to abandon principle? Forbid it, Almighty God! Paralyzed be the Baptist hand that reaches that bread and wine over one of God's limitations, and "to the roof of his mouth may the tongue of that Baptist cleave," who gives an invitation broader than the warrant of God. The ground is perilous and borders on rebellion and blasphemy. Listen to the Scriptures:

"Whatsoever thing I command you observe to do it. Thou shalt not add thereto nor diminish therefrom," Deut. 12:32. "Add not then to His work, lest He reprove thee and thou be found a liar," Prov. 30:6. "Teaching them to observe all things whatsoever I have commanded you," Matt. 28:30. "If ye love me, keep my commandments. * * * Ye are my friends if you do whatsoever I command you."

Of the Pharisee, Jesus said: "In vain do they worship me, teaching for doctrines the commandments of men. For laying aside the commandment of God ye hold the tradition of men. * * * Making the word of God of none effect through your tradition." Mark 7:2-13.

Upon the same subject Paul wrote: "Wherefore, if ye be dead with Christ from the rudiments of the world, are ye subject to ordinances after the commandments and doctrines of men? Which things have indeed a show of wisdom in willworship and humility, etc. Touch not, taste not, handle not, which all are to perish with the using," Substantially Col. 2:20-23.

In allowing a sickly sentimentality, an affectation of charity to transport us beyond a divine requirement, we may expect the chiding God's prophet gave to Saul: "Who hath required this at your hands?" Of such a one the Lord Himself asks: "Why do you call me Lord, Lord, and do not the things I command?" Again He says: "Wherefore, whosoever shall break one of these least commandments and shall teach men so, he shall be called the least in the kingdom of heaven."

These scriptures establish broad principles. From them we deduce the doctrines that human traditions respecting any ordinance of God if (a) mere will-worship; (b) impugns the

A Discussion of the Lord's Supper

authority of God; (c) makes void His law; (d) perishes with the using; (e) that such traditions we are to touch not, taste not, handle not. (f) That he who teaches them diminishes his importance in the kingdom of heaven.

If a man be on the rock Christ Jesus, that only foundation, he will be saved. But if he build upon that foundation wood, hay and stubble, in the *fiery* ordeal through which all men's actions must pass, *his works will be burned up* and *he shall suffer loss*. But the man himself, if on the rock, shall be saved, "though as it were by fire," I Cor. 3:11-15.

These scriptures and principles apply to Baptists as well as others. If it is our people holding traditions and making void the law of God, their works will be burned up. Brethren, forget not the day of trial—the ordeal of fire. But if Baptist principles be correct then OPEN COMMUNION MAKES VOID THE LAW OF GOD, in the following particulars:

1. The bread and wine are given to some who do not even profess conversion. To those who are unbaptized. To some who are under church censure and who have been disciplined. As far as the subjects _are concerned, the law of God is thus made void in three specifications.

2. The object God had in view is "laid aside." He said, "This do in remembrance of me." Open communion invites the unconverted to commune "as a means of grace." Sometimes it is said, "If ever I was converted in the world, it was in the act of communing," thus making a mere emblem a converting agency and glorifying an act of rebellion.

Open communion loses sight of God's object in being administered to show fellowship for other denominations. The Savior said, "This do in remembrance of me." Fellowship among denominations is a great thing, but if the shadow of our coming together darkens the cross of Calvary, and causes us to lose sight of the Redeemer, then, O mighty God, *keep us forever apart!*

Open communion is observed sometimes that husband and wife, belonging to different organizations, may eat at the same sacramental table. When two are agreed it is well to see them walk together. The Word of God commands the husband to love his wife even as his own body. Let him love her, guard her from peril and make all his faculties the servants of his love in her behalf. Let her be dearer than all the world to him. But, O husband, exalt her not above God! Why should "a man's foes be those of his own household?" Thy wife may be wondrously fair, but though the orange bloom be fresh in her hair, let her not be obtruded before a dying Savior! In communion He says, "Remember me"—not your wife. 'Tis not the time to think of her. Scourged from our hearts in that hallowed hour be every image but that dear face, "marred" for us "more than that of any of the sons of men."

3. Open communion makes void the law of God in setting His table out of His kingdom. He said: "I appoint unto you a kingdom, to eat and to drink, at my table, *in my kingdom.*" Open communion gives the bread and wine to some who have never been baptized, or who have been excluded from the church. For when a man is excluded from one denomination, he has only to join another, and then come to that table from which he had been expelled.

That emphatic triple prohibition of Paul, "Touch not, taste not, handle not," is far more pertinent to this subject than to the drinking of ardent spirits. It has no direct reference to whiskey-drinking, but primarily refers to something even more obnoxious to God's law, i.e., to partaking of "ordinances after the commandments and traditions of man." It is a downright close communion text.

If, as they confidently believe, the Baptists hold the traditions, it says to all Pedo-Baptists desiring to approach our communion table, *"Touch not, taste not, handle not."* If, as we confidently believe, they are making void God's law by their traditions, it comes like the point of a two-edged sword to the heart of the open communion Baptist, "TOUCH NOT, TASTE NOT, HANDLE NOT." We therefore cherish the conviction that no just censure attaches to the Baptist practice because it is the Lord's table. Let us then, in our search for "Baptist bigotry," examine another query

Are Baptists bigoted because they make baptism a prerequisite to communion? Let an appeal be made to the Word of God. From that holy book we learn:

1. *That baptism was first appointed and practiced.*

The first baptizer never saw the communion table. Jesus Himself was baptized, then made and baptized disciples, long before He Himself commanded or appointed communion for others. See John 3:22, 23 and 4:1; Matt. 26:26.

2. *First in the commission.*

"Go teach all nations, baptizing them in the name of the Father, the Son and Holy Spirit, teaching them to observe all things whatsoever I have commanded you," Matt. 28:20. Here the order of the commandment is (a) make disciples, (b) baptize them, (c) teach them to commune. For communion is one of the things He had commanded them to observe.

3. *We find that the apostles so understood this order by their practice.*

Take the first instance, with which all the rest harmonize. On the day of Pentecost Peter preached a sermon. The people were convicted and said, "What must we do?" The apostle replied, "Repent and be baptized," etc. Then the record says, "They that gladly received the word were baptized," and then adds, "They continued steadfastly in the apostles' doctrine and fellowship and *breaking of bread,*" etc. Acts 2:3840. Even a child can see that the people were baptized before they communed.

4. *In instructing the churches the connection shows that baptism was first.*

Take one instance as an illustration—that one most relied on by open communionists. It is that much quoted Scripture, "Let a man examine himself and so let him eat." By this Scripture they seek to prove that the individual and not the church must judge. Ten thousand times it has been quoted in triumph, as if it were the "end of the controversy."

Let us fairly test this invincible (?) argument. *Unto whom was this language addressed?* To everybody? Where do we find the language, "Let a man examine himself and so let him eat"? It is found in I Cor. 11:28. What do we know about these Corinthians to whom Paul was writing? Turn to Acts 18:1-11: "After these things Paul came to Corinth—and reasoned in the synagogue—and Crispus, the chief ruler of the synagogue, believed on the Lord with all his house; *and many of the Corinthians hearing believed and were baptized.*" This is the account of their baptism.

Now mark the beginning of that letter in which the expression occurs: "Paul, called to be an apostle of Jesus Christ, through the will of God, and Sosthenes our brother, *unto the church of God, which is at Corinth,"* etc. This shows that they were organized into a church. Finally, examine carefully the very chapter in which the expression occurs, and you will find (I Cor. 11:18, 20, 22, 23) that when assembled together, in one place, in church capacity, then, and only then, it is said to these baptized Corinthians, "Let a man examine himself and so let him eat of that bread and drink of that cup." It is a perversion of the Word of God to make this justify open communion.

5. *The scriptures make baptism the initiatory ordinance.*

It is the emblem of the beginning of spiritual life. Communion is the emblem of the nutrition of that life. Shall we reverse the analogy of nature and adopt the absurdity that food must be given to the non-existent?

6. *There is some analogy between the Lord's supper and the Jewish passover; and some analogy between circumcision*

A Discussion of the Lord's Supper

and baptism, though baptism did not come in the place of circumcision.

The Jewish law was explicit (Exodus 12:4$) "No uncircumcised man must eat thereof," and following the analogy, and in the language of a distinguished Methodist, "No unbaptized man must eat of the Lord's Supper."

All Baptists make these arguments from the Scriptures; but they do not stand alone in thus interpreting the Word of God. It is common ground, for, ALL DENOMINATIONS TEACH THAT BAPTISM MUST PRECEDE COMMUNION. And every denomination determines for itself what is baptism. I submit, as a fair sample of a great mass of testimony, the following:

Wall (noted Pedo-Baptist historian), in his "History of Infant Baptism," Part II, Chapter 19, says: "No church ever gave the communion to any persons before they were baptized.

Among all the absurdities that ever were held, none ever maintained that any person should partake of the communion before he was baptized."

To the same effect speaks Dr. Doddridge, "Lectures," page 511: "As far as our knowledge of primitive antiquity teaches, it is certain that no unbaptized person ever received the Lord's Supper."

Note again the testimony of Dr. Timothy Dwight, President of Yale College: "It is an indispensable qualification for this ordinance that the candidate for communion be a member of the visible church of Christ, in full standing. By this I intend that he shall be a person of piety; that he should have made a public profession of religion; and that he should have been baptized."

The only scriptural grounds on which any minister can invite other denominations to commune is that they are members of the church of Christ and baptized. The denial of this necessarily precludes communion. As proof, I submit the following quotations from Dr. O. Fisher, the great Methodist baptismal debater:

"The Baptists, setting themselves up for the only right ones holding all others as out of the church, because unbaptized, they themselves are after all proved to be just what they have held others to be, unbaptized, as they certainly have neither the mode nor design of baptism, and have only a part of its subjects. And it may be seriously questioned whether the baptism administered by our Baptist brethren, holding the views they do respecting it, ought to be received as valid by the other evangelical churches, and *therefore—whether it be truly and strictly lawful to hold communion with them, even where they are willing.*" ("Christian Sacraments," section "History of Immersion"—pages 184, 185).

This then is the true issue: What is a visible church of Christ? What is baptism? Never, while remains the testimony of Mark, that "John baptized the people in the river of Jordan"; never, while Enon, the place of much water, remains in the bible; never, while it is said "that Philip and the Eunuch both went down into the water"; never while the record of our blessed Savior's baptism remains, concerning whom it is said, "When He was baptized He came up straightway out of the water," and with whom, Paul says, "we are buried in baptism"; never, while these remain, will Baptists concede that moistening the forehead from a pitcher is baptism; and so never can invite with consistency the Pedo-Baptists to communion with them.

Since the great principles which underlie the communion question are held in common by all denominations, to all the fair-minded and candid I submit the question: Is it right to attribute our practice to bigotry? Let a great Methodist historian answer. Hibbard, in his "History of Methodism," says:

"It is but just to remark that in one principle the Baptist and Pedo-Baptist churches agree. They both agree in rejecting

A Discussion of the Lord's Supper

from communion at the table of the Lord, and in denying the right of church fellowship to all who have not been baptized. Valid baptism they consider as essential to constitute visible church membership. This also we hold. The only question, then, that divides us is: What is essential to valid baptism? The Baptists, in passing a sweeping sentence of disfranchisement upon all the Christian churches, have only acted upon a principle held in common with all other Christian churches, viz: That baptism is essential to church membership. They have denied our baptism and, as unbaptized persons, we have been excluded from their table. That they greatly err in their views of Christian baptism we, of course, believe. But according to their view of baptism, they certainly are consistent in restricting this their communion. We would not be understood as passing a judgment of approval upon their course; but we may say their views of baptism force them upon the ground of strict communion and herein they act upon the same principles as other churches. They admit only those whom they deem baptized persons to the communion table. Of course they must be their own judges as to what baptism is. It is evident that according to our views we can admit them to our *communion;* but with their views of baptism, it is equally evident they can never reciprocate the courtesy; and the charge of *close communion* is no more applicable to the Baptists than to us; insomuch that the question of church membership is determined by as liberal principles as it is with any other Protestant churches—so far, I mean, as the present subject is concerned, *i.e.,* it is determined by valid baptism."

Will my Methodist brethren allow me to call special attention to this extract? They have no greater man than Hibbard, of New York, and very few of his equal in candor. The points to which attention is especially directed are as follows:

1. He says that Baptists, in determining church membership, are governed by as liberal principles as any other

church. No bigotry there.

2. The charge of close communion is no more applicable to them than to Pedo-Baptist churches. No bigotry there.

3. In making baptism precede communion, they act on principles shared by all Pedo-Baptist churches. No bigotry there.

4. The Baptists are consistent in their restricted communion. No illiberality there.

5. They must be their own judges as to what baptism is.

6. The only question that divides us is, What is valid baptism?

Will our brethren of other denominations follow this magnanimous leader and do us common justice at least? And since they hold baptism as an indispensable prerequisite to communion, I have another question to ask them: Is it right or fair to quote Robert Hall, the open communion Baptist, against us, since they despise his premise? Do they really respect his position? Listen to his words, and as they love his conclusion, let them accept his premise. Either retain both or reject both. He says:

"We certainly make no scruple in informing a Pedo-Baptist candidate that we consider him as unbaptized, and disdain all concealment on the subject. If we supposed there were a necessary, unalterable connection between the two positive Christian institutes, so that none were qualified for communion who had not been previously baptized, we could not hesitate for a moment respecting the refusal of Pedo-Baptists, without renouncing the principles of our denomination." Vol. I, pages 403 and 445, Hall's works.

In other places he argues for open communion on the ground of human weakness, their weakness in the faith. Thus we see that Robert Hall receives Pedo-Baptists to the communion only on two grounds:

A Discussion of the Lord's Supper

(1) That baptism is not essential to communion.

(2) In condescension to their weakness.

Let us propound yet other queries: Are Baptists censurable in making the church and not the individual the judge of external qualification? By external qualification I mean a credible profession of religion, baptism, church connection and orderly walk.

When God sent out His ministers to disciple the nations, do you suppose that Paul or john or Peter ever left it to the candidates to say what was baptism, or for what purpose they were baptized? Were a group of converts left free to determine the form of church government? Or did the apostles go out discipling according to the Savior's method, *baptizing* as He was baptized, and organizing churches according to the Divine model? Let candor and common sense answer. But whatever may be the scriptural argument, as long as their position is the same as ours, let them pass no censures.

Just here the question will arise in the Baptist mind, Why this late war on the communion question? It is not the ancient battleground. There are men living, nearly old enough to remember when communion with Baptists was never sought—when Baptists were not accredited worthy to commune at their table. Stripes and fagots have given place to kisses and embraces.

Again the question recurs, growing mightier and more massive from every consideration of the past, Why is the battleground shifted, and the weapons of warfare changed? Baptists believe it is because Pedo-Baptists have been driven to the wall on the baptismal question. They are profoundly conscious that the young convert, unbiased by prejudice, finds in his Bible that the Savior was immersed. That he ought to follow Christ. And all the power of childish associations, and all the memories of father and mother are not sufficient to make this convert believe in infant baptism. He wants to be baptized for himself, and upon a profession of his own faith. How shall he be hindered?

By presenting to his heart, all aglow with the freshness of love, close communion all invested with horror. By darkening it with epithets and clothing it in mantles of bigotry and intolerance. What community has not its adept in this work? But after Hibbard and men like him have spoken, surely none but the ignorant, or those blinded by prejudice, or those thoroughly carried away by the popular clamor for charity, will continue the work of misrepresentation and darkening counsel.

But are Baptists censurable for refusing to make this ordinance a means of exhibiting Christian fellowship for other denominations? Are we driven to such straits to show our Christian love, that an ordinance of God must be perverted? Is the arena for the exhibition of Christian charity so circumscribed as to warrant such a report? Is the field of Christian co-operation so narrow that we must have recourse to such an expedient? How many times must it be repeated, that in communion the local congregation of Baptist believers, assembled together in one place as a church, as a bride, "remembers Jesus, the absent husband, and shows forth His death until He comes"? All other objects of communion are foreign to God's one, original purpose. In prayer, by the bedside of the dying, in life's multiform battles, we can evidence our love and Christian fellowship.

BUT DOES NOT CLOSE COMMUNION UNCHRISTIANIZE OTHER DENOMINATIONS? No true Baptist ever believed it or taught it. Baptists, alone, of all denominations, can clearly show that their standard works teach that neither baptism nor communion is essential to salvation. Their uniform doctrine has been salvation essential to baptism. They have ever been taught that "whosoever believeth in the Lord Jesus Christ hath everlasting life, and shall not come into condemnation." That even out of Rome, "the mother of harlots," will God call many of His people.

A Discussion of the Lord's Supper

But one single fact settles this question forever. Here on my left sits a brother whom we have just received. He is adjudged a Christian by the unanimous vote of the church. He is to be baptized this evening. And yet, until baptized, our communion table is closed against him. We believe him to be as much baptized as any Pedo-Baptist. *Shall we allow more privileges to other denominations than to those converts received for our baptism?*

But more to the point: Does our close communion un-christianize this brother, who, by the undivided voice of the church, has been declared a Christian? If our reason has not lost its balance, we must answer, No! There can be no sectarian bigotry here. Where then in our practice shall it be found?

Is there any force in that threadbare statement—that hackneyed phrase—"WE SHALL COMMUNE TOGETHER IN HEAVEN, WHY NOT ON EARTH?" This is one of the sophisms referred to. All great logicians, Aristotle, Hedge, Whately and others, unite in anathematizing the sophist.

Surely if an attorney-at-law is disgraced who wilfully uses a sophism to gain a case, no man can be held guiltless who uses one in religious controversy. Under the fair surface of this much quoted and popular expression there lurks a fallacy. But little attention is necessary to point it out. It is the use of the same word in both premise and conclusion, when the word has a very different meaning in the one form from what it does in the other. It is the word COMMUNION. The premise is—"We shall all commune together in heaven." The conclusion is—"Therefore we should all commune together on earth." The communion referred to on earth is a communion of bread and wine. The communion in heaven referred to is a spiritual communion. No one expects a communion table of bread and wine to be set in heaven, because such communion expires with the coming of the Savior. He says, "Ye do show the Lord's death until He come." The earthly communion table has fulfilled its mission when Shiloh comes again.

In order for premise and conclusion to harmonize and the one to necessarily flow from the other, the meaning of the word must be the same in both. If our Pedo-Baptist brethren say, "We shall all hold *spiritual* communion in heaven, therefore we ought to have spiritual communion on earth," we accept the conclusion, and claim that we do have with all Christians Christian fellowship and spiritual communion, as the whole world knows.

But if they say, "All denominations will gather around one communion table of bread and wine in heaven, just such one as we have here, therefore the earthly practice should conform to the heavenly," we reply:

(1) The premise is false, as it is not in evidence from the Bible that there will be such a table set.

(2) Even if the premise is true, the conclusion does not follow, because in heaven, if we ever get there, we shall all have one faith and shall have left behind us in the ashes of the great conflagration those differences which necessitate different tables here.

Thus the emptiness and fallacy of this redoubted sophism is made manifest; but let us put the question to them: Do they receive all to their communion table whom the Lord proposes to save? Is this their law of communion? All whom Jesus receives? They make no pretension to it. Brethren of other denominations, all of you who love justice and truth, I make my appeal to you—Is that man guiltless before God who, to the detriment of another denomination, perpetrates this sophism? If to pervert Scripture be criminal, how much more to misuse the heavenly glory?

Is there any force in the objection that *close communion separates members of the same family from the same sacramental table?* In the first place, if close communion is of divine appointment, it is not the separating power. God said

A Discussion of the Lord's Supper

to the Jews, "Your sins have separated between you and me." It was not the law that separated, but sin. Law was ordained to life. Its purpose was to bind to God. But transgression may make that which was ordained to life a means of death. See Paul's argument—Romans 7. There is, however, a secondary sense in which it divides families or arrays them against each other, so that "a man's foes are those of his own household." But whatever of force there is in this objection against restricted communion applies with equal power against the Christian religion.

Our Savior says: "Think not that I am come to send peace on the earth; I came not to send peace but a sword. For I am come to set a man at variance against his father, and the daughter against her mother, and the daughter-in-law against her mother-in-law. And a man's foes shall be they of his own household. He that loveth father or mother more than me is not worthy of me. And he that taketh not his cross and followeth after me is not worthy of me." See Matt. 10:34-39.

This was the very objection the enemy used against the Christian religion: "They are come here also who have turned the world upside down."

In these latter days religion is wounded in the house of its friends. Principle is sacrificed to convenience and pleasure, and family relations are exalted above God's Word. The dignity and majesty of law is sold out to gratify human passions and to conciliate the world. How often you hear it: "Join that church where you can enjoy your religion the best." "You had better go along with your wife or your husband or father." As if our enjoyment had anything to do with it. 0 God, send thy Spirit to impress us, until we ask no longer, "What will I enjoy? What will please my husband or wife?" but *"What wilt thou have me to do?"*

In the next place let us inquire: IS CLOSE COMMUNION A BAR TO CHRISTIAN UNION? I know that this charge is made all over the land. Papers that profess to be non-sectarian thus covertly thrust at our beloved principles. The pulpit, the press, the parlor and the kitchen unite in the declaration. The impression is made that if it were not for "those bigoted, close communion Baptists," the Protestant world would be a unit. Now, is there a shadow of truth in this assumption? If facts ever did explode a fallacy, they have burst this air-bubble. Facts! Yes, well-established, stubborn facts give it the lie.

If close communion were the bar to Christian union, then where there is no close communion there would be Christian union. But let one solitary instance stand up as a colossal monument sublimely protesting against this phantom of the brain. Let it be written in broad capitals over ever communion table:

CHARLES H. SPURGEON WAS DEBARRED FROM THE BRITISH EVANGELICAL ALLIANCE AND IN CONSEQUENCE FROM THE WORLD'S EVANGELICAL ALLIANCE!

Yes, the world's greatest and most influential open communion Baptist, a man whose pulpit efficiency, whose height and depth of influence have had no equal since the Apostle Paul, this man representing the open communion Baptist churches of England had no part in the far-famed World's Evangelical Alliance, while J.L.M. Curry, the silver-tongued orator of the close communion Baptists, not only held in that august body an honorable position, but made before it the grandest speech delivered at its late session in the United States!

"O Temporal O Mores!" Did Spurgeon's open communion sentiments save him? No. Do they exempt him from Pedo-Baptist onslaught? Nay, verily. Exists there as much Christian union between him and the open communion churches and the Pedo-Baptists of England, as between the Pedo-Baptists and the close communion Baptist churches of

A Discussion of the Lord's Supper

America? Most certainly not. The fact is, open communion forfeits rather than secures Pedo-Baptist regard.

In going to the table of another denomination, a Baptist makes the fatal concession that it is the church of Jesus Christ and its members baptized. Making this, it *is his duty to join* it. The assumption that close communion is the bar to Christian union is as unsubstantial as an idle dream, a hallucination lighter than a gulf cloud.

But I have yet other questions to urge: Do Pedo-Baptists regard Baptists as acting conscientiously in their communion views? If not, how dare they invite to God's table those whom they regard as unprincipled and unconscientious? If they do, how can they have the face to ask a fellow Christian to violate the promptings of his conscience? Upon which horn of the dilemma do they desire to be impaled?

Yet again: As they admit our baptism and church membership, and can therefore, as far as that is concerned, invite us to commune with them without violation of conscience, and as we do not admit their baptism or church connection, and cannot therefore invite them without violation of conscience, where is our illiberality? Where is the bigotry? The principle on which both proceed is precisely the same.

Let me ask the fair-minded and candid among them to show me a way out of this dilemma: Shall I invite them to the communion as baptized? This stultifies my principles. Shall I invite them as unbaptized? They themselves regard this as rebellion against God. What kind of an invitation would they have, an honest or a dishonest one? If it be dishonest, who shall answer for us to God? If honest, will they accept? How much would they be flattered with such an invitation as this, and how much would it recommend us:

"Brethren Pedo-Baptists, we do not regard you as baptized; we agree with you that baptism is necessary to communion, but respecting your views more than our conscience or the Word of God, we ask you to come along with us to the communion table. We do not regard it as appointed to show Christian fellowship, nor to unite husband and wife, nor as a means of grace, but in deference to your superior judgment we yield these matters." Who of them would accept the invitation thus given?

And now to my own brethren I turn, with the question: DOES OPEN COMMUNION HAVE A TENDENCY TO PROSPER AND PERPETUATE BAPTIST CHURCHES? As an answer,

(a) Look to the melancholy history of John Bunyan's church. He stood out with Robert Hall as one of the champions of open communion. He believed, preached and practiced it. How did it affect his church? After his death, Pedo-Baptists claimed that they had the right to vote as well as to commune. As none could consistently deny it, they exercised that right, and for a hundred years put Pedo-Baptist preachers in old John Bunyan's pulpit and pastorate. From 1688 to 1788, no Baptist preacher was pastor. And when the last of these pastors was converted to the Baptist faith, he was retained only on the condition that he would not preach on baptism.

He was gagged in his own house. Yes, open communion throttled him and made him keep back part of the counsel of God. In 1700, and again in 1724, they refused to grant letters to their members desiring to unite with close communion churches.

Open communion is to Baptists what the Trojan horse made by Greeks was to Troy. It pretended to be an offering to the immortal gods. But it was made so large that the walls had to be broken down for its reception, and in its cavernous interior many of the bravest Greeks were concealed.

(b) Look next to the fading glories of the Free-will Baptists, and last

(c) to the shameful downfall of Dr. Pentecost. But yesterday

A Discussion of the Lord's Supper

he cast a shadow across a continent—now none so poor to do him honor.

The prosperity of Spurgeon's church is attributable to the fact that their open communion has never had a chance (and could not in his lifetime) to be carried to its legitimate consequences. Wait until, like Bunyan, he has been sleeping one hundred years, then read the history.

Again: DOES OPEN COMMUNION ENABLE BAPTISTS TO MAKE CONVERTS MORE RAPIDLY OF PEDO-BAPTISTS? As a test, take an instance: The Rev. John Foster, of London, left his church to accept the call of the Independent Church at Piner's Hall. But though for years their pastor, he never baptized one of them. They, of course, concluded that if he would accept the pastoral-care of their church, they were near enough right. If you ever want to convert PedoBaptists, make no compromise with their errors.

But does the avowal of open communion sentiments and the most earnest invitations for intercommunion ever secure much of it?

No Pedo-Baptist regularly communed with Robert Hall's open communion church. It existed in name almost altogether. Inter-communion with Spurgeon's church was infrequent, and never, except in the case of isolated individuals. It is beyond my knowledge if there was ever any church communion in his case. It is known that Pedo-Baptists do not throng the tables of the Free-will Baptists. And how long and how far did they follow the misguided Pentecost? It is either a fruitless theory, or the fruits are apples from Sodom for Baptists. I desire to stand by the old landmark today and lift a voice of warning to my brethren—OPEN COMMUNION IS THE ENTERING WEDGE OF DEATH TO OUR CHURCHES.

The kiss of intercommunion is as the kiss of Judas, and their embrace the embrace of death. In preference, give us back the fagot, the dungeon and the martyr fires. These were the portions of Baptists not many years ago. No Pedo-Baptist denomination sought communion with us then. Read the history of ecclesiastical affairs in the reign of Elizabeth, and since that time. If my statement is questioned, let me be put to the proof.

What, then, should be done with the Baptist minister who preaches and practices open communion? If he be an Apollos in eloquence, a Rothschild in wealth, or a Jesse Mercer in influence, let his name be blotted from our records. He costs us far too much to retain him. We cannot pay the price of existence for the honor of having him among us.

What shall be done with a private member who practices open communion? If he be sound in the faith in other particulars, kindly admonish him and have patience with him, that you may gain your brother. Show him how it is far better to comply with the genius and rules of his church. Bear with him. But if he persists, the welfare of the church imperatively demands his expulsion. He is walking disorderly. Let the fellowship of the church be withdrawn from him. If he is sincere, if he is conscientious and determined in his practice, his common sense, as well as our discipline, will show him that the Baptist church is no place for him. If he persists for popular effect, for any unworthy, time-serving motive, he is unworthy of membership in any church. Politics as well as religion might well unite in the prayer, *"From all trimmers,* Good Lord, deliver us!"

Those of our brethren who are Baptists upon all other points, and simply have doubts upon the communion question, and who do not purpose practising open communion, nor propagating it, but can conscientiously comply with the church regulations, had better remain in the Baptist church, because

(1) in going to another church they do not secure open *communion,* since by going they lose Baptist communion and

(2) in joining a Pedo-Baptist organization they will have to

A Discussion of the Lord's Supper

endorse and support many things obnoxious to their faith.

It certainly is passing strange that for the sake of anything so empty of practical good as open communion, a man will give up his convictions—

(1) That immersion alone is baptism.

(2) That believers only are subjects of baptism.

(3) That the church of Jesus Christ is a democracy.

And now in all kindness let me once more impress upon the minds of my brethren THE SIN OF OPEN COMMUNION. At the bar of God's truth I impeach it of sin and of treason, because—

(1) It violates the law of God making it a church ordinance. They set their table "out of the Kingdom."

(2) It is a sin, because it gives the bread and wine to the unconverted.

(3) It is a sin because given to the unbaptized.

(4) I impeach it of the sin of substitution. God's reason for communion is superseded, and it is received to show Christian fellowship and to unite husband and wife.

(5) It is treason, in that it makes *void the law of discipline.*

(6) It is sin in being used "as a means of grace."

(7) It is a sin in that it seeks the destruction of Baptist churches.

(8) It is a sin, in that it is founded upon a sickly sentimentality, an affected charity, and upon fallacies and sophisms, and teems with glaring inconsistencies. In all the universe of created things, animate and inanimate, it has no counterpart. It stands before us like Nebuchadnezzar's dream.

"Thou, O King, sawest and beheld a great image. This great image, whose brightness was excellent, stood before thee. And the form thereof was terrible. This image's head was of fine gold, his breasts and his arms of silver, his body and his thighs of brass, his legs of iron, his feet part of iron and part of clay."

Such is its picture, and, as in the case of that other image set up by Nebuchadnezzar, the whole world is called upon to fall down and worship it, and "wonder at the beast with a great admiration." This luminous, this terrible image! Who can stand before it?

"Thou sawest till that a stone was cut out without hands, which smote the image upon its feet, that were of iron and clay, (which could not cleave to one another), and brake them in pieces. Then was the iron, the clay, the brass, the silver and the gold broken to pieces together, and became like the chaff of the summer threshing floors; and the wind carried them away, that no place was found for them: and the stone that smote the image became a great mountain and filled the whole earth."

So the truth of God smites the great image of open communion upon its earthen foundation, and shivers into countless fragments its incoherent particles.

DISTINCTIVE BAPTIST PRINCIPLES

DISTINCTIVE BAPTIST PRINCIPLES.[1]

TEXT—"A declaration of those things which are most surely believed among us"—Luke 1:1. "It was needful for me * * to exhort you that you should earnestly contend for the *faith* which was once delivered to the saints."—Jude 3.

THE distinctive principles of the Baptists are those doctrines or practices which distinguish us from other Christian denominations. It is held by some that no doctrine or practice should be classed as *distinctive* which has at any time been shared, in whole or in part, by any other denomination. But this limited sense of the word distinctive is too narrow for ordinary speech or common sense. For example: The Greek Church and the Baptists both practice immersion, but their doctrine of baptism is widely different from ours. Authority, subject, and design all enter as much into the validity of this ordinance as the act itself. More than mere immersion is necessary to constitute New Testament baptism. Again, the Congregationalists agree with Baptists in the form of church government, but their doctrine of the church is widely different from ours. Yet again, the

---

[1] Carroll, B. H. *Baptists and Their Doctrines.* Comp., J. B. Cranfill. Philadelphia: American Baptist Publication Society, 1913. 7-36. A Sermon Preached before the Pastor's Conference in Dallas, Texas, November 4, 1903. Published by Unanimous Request of the Conference.

statement of Chillingworth, "The Bible, and the Bible alone, the religion of Protestants," is widely different from the Baptist principle, "The New Testament, the only law of Christianity."

Moreover, this entire subject has an historic aspect, which may not be ignored. There has been great progress in Baptist principles since the Reformation of the sixteenth century. Throughout the Protestant world there has been steady approximation by nearly all other denominations to many Baptist principles, very materially narrowing the once broad margin dividing us from other people. So that the distinctive in *history* is much more marked than the distinctive of the present day. Notable among the Baptist doctrines towards which there has been this steady approximation are "Freedom of Conscience" and "Separation of Church and State." It is one of the best established facts of history that Protestants equally with Romanists once held to the unchristian and horrible maxim "Whose is the government—his is the religion." Geneva, Germany, Holland, Old England, and New England shared it with Italy, Spain, and France, as Baptists found to their cost. While, therefore, the more recent approximations towards our principles, are warmly welcomed, and while the hope of still greater approximation is fondly cherished, we are not thereby estopped from entrance into the domain of history in discussing distinctive principles.

Before coming to affirmative statements, allow me to clear away the brush obstructing a fair view by disclaiming as *distinctive* the only two doctrines which in the world's estimation constitute the sum of our distinctive principles

(1) Immersion is Baptism.

Immersion is not disclaimed as a Baptist doctrine, but it is disclaimed as a distinctive tenet. Think of it. For the first thirteen hundred years all Christendom held this belief. Even today other Christian denominations, aggregating nearly one hundred million people, believe and practice it as the only baptism. How, then, can it be our most distinguishing tenet? If, indeed, it be distinctive of our people, it is the least distinctive and the least important of all our principles. In this discussion it will not even be named as a distinctive principle.

(2) BAPTISM IS ESSENTIAL TO SALVATION.

So far from being distinctive this is not now and never has been a Baptist doctrine. More than all other people do they repudiate it. Indeed, on the contrary, the Baptists are the only people in the world who hold its exact opposite: *Salvation is essential to baptism.*

On these premises and disclaimers we may now announce, in order, the distinctive Baptist principles.

I. THE NEW TESTAMENT—THE LAW OF CHRISTIANITY.

Doubtless many of my fellow Christians of other denominations may be disposed to smile at the announcement of this as a distinctive Baptist principle. But let us not smile too soon. Patiently await the development of the thought. To expand the statement All the New Testament is the Law of Christianity. The New Testament is all the Law of Christianity. The New Testament will always be all the Law of Christianity. This does not deny the inspiration or profit of the Old Testament; nor that the New is a development of the Old. It affirms, however, that the Old Testament, as a typical, educational, and transitory system was fulfilled in Christ, and as a standard of law and way of life was nailed to the cross of Christ and so taken out of the way. The principle teaches that we should not go to the Old Testament to find Christian law or Christian institutions. Not there do we find the true idea of the Christian church, or its members, or its ordinances, or its government, or its officers, or its sacrifices, or its worship, or its mission, or its ritual, or its priesthood. Now, when we consider the fact that the overwhelming majority of Christendom today, whether Greek, Romanist or Protestant, borrow from the Old Testament so much of their doctrine of the church, including its members, officers, ritual, ordinances, government, liturgy, and mission, we may well call this a distinctive Baptist principle. This is not a question of what is the Bible. If it were, Baptists would not be distinguished from many Protestants in rejecting the apochryphal additions incorporated by Romanists in their Old Testament. Nor is it a stand with Chillingworth on the proposition, "The Bible, and the Bible alone, the religion of Protestants." If it were, Baptists would not be distinguished from many Protestants in rejecting the equal authority of tradition as held by the Romanists. But when Baptists say that the New Testament is the only law for Christian institutions they part company, if not theoretically at least practically, with most of the Protestant world, as well as from the Greeks and Romanists. We believe that the church, with all that pertains to it, is strictly a New Testament institution. We do not deny that there was an Old Testament *ecclesia,* but do deny its identity with the New Testament *ecclesia.* We do not deny the circumcision of infants under Old Testament law, but do deny their baptism under New Testament law. We do not deny that there were elders under the Mosaic economy, nor even deny the facts of uninspired history concerning the elders of the Jewish synagogue. We simply claim that the New Testament alone must define the office and functions of the elder in the Christian church. Christ himself appointed its Apostles and its first seventy elders. We not only stand upon the New Testament alone in repelling Old Testament institutions, in repelling apocryphal additions thereto, in repelling the historic synagogue of the inter-biblical period as the model of the church, but to repel the binding authority of post-apostolic history, whether embodied in the literature of the ante Nicene fathers or in the decisions of councils, from the council at Nice, A.D. 325, to the Vatican Council, A. D. 1870. We allow not Clement, Polycarp, Hippolytus, Ignatius, Irenaeus, Justin, Tertullian, Cyprian, Origen, Jerome, Eusebius, Augustine, Chrysostom, Erasmus, Luther, Zwingli, Calvin, Henry VIII, Knox, or Wesley either to determine what is New Testament law or to make law for us. In determining the office and functions of a bishop, we consider neither the Septuagint *episcopos,* nor the Gentile *episcopos,* nor the developed *episcopos of* the early Christian centuries.

Distinctive Baptist Principles

We shut ourselves up to the New Testament teaching concerning the bishop. But recently the Christian world has been invited to unite on the historic episcopacy of the early Christian centuries. We made no response to this unscriptural invitation. Yet more recently, the eccentric, and I may add, the heretical, higher critic, Dr. Briggs, seeks, it seems, to unite the Christian world on the word katholikos (universal) as applied to the church and as defined in these same early Christian centuries. We utterly disregard this invitation, not only because his word *katholikos* is found nowhere in the Greek of either Old or New Testament, but because the idea of catholicity must not be learned from post-apostolic fathers, but from the inspired New Testament, and because it was this word, katholikos, which led to the idea of the church as an organized general body having appellate jurisdiction over the particular congregations, and led to the union of Church and State under Constantine. We are willing enough to enter the domain of uninspired history as a matter of research, and ready enough to concede all its fairly established facts, whatever sound proof may show them to be, but we recognize as the only ground of union, now or hereafter, the impregnable rock of the New Testament.

And mark you the first form of the expanded statement: All the New Testament is the law of Christianity. To apply this thought One Christian denomination, in determining the law of pardon, would shut us out of the four Gospel narratives up to the resurrection of Christ and shut us up to the latter half of the New Testament. Here we say, give us all the New Testament. The cases of forgiveness of sin, at the mouth and hand of our Lord himself, must be considered in determining the law of pardon.

The New Testament is the law of Christianity. All the *Now* Testament is the law of Christianity. The New Testament is all the law of Christianity. The New Testament always will be all the law of Christianity. Avaunt ye types and shadows! Avaunt Apochrypha! Avaunt O Synagogue! Avaunt Tradition, thou boar-headed liar! Hush! Be still and listen! All through the Christian apes—from dark and noisome dungeons, from the lone wanderings of banishment and expatriation, from the roarings and sickening conflagrations of martyr fires—there comes a voice shouted here, whispered there, sighed, sobbed, or gasped elsewhere a Baptist voice, clearer than a silver trumpet and sweeter than the chime of bells, a voice that freights and glorifies the breeze or gale that bears it. O Earth, hearken to it: *The New Testament is the law of Christianity!* Let the disciples of Zoroaster, Brahma, Confucius, Zeno, and Epicures hear it. And when Mahomet comes with his Koran, or Joe Smith with his book of Mormon, or Swedenborg with his new revelations, or spirit-rappers, wizards, witches, and necromancers with their impostures, confront each in turn with the all-sufficient revelation of this book, and when science—falsely so called (properly speculative philosophy)—would hold up the book as moribund, effete, or obsolete, may that Baptist voice rebuke it. Christ himself set up His kingdom. Christ himself established His church. Christ himself gave us Christian law. And the men whom He inspired furnish us the only reliable record of these institutions. They had no successors in inspiration. The record is complete. Prophecy and vision have ceased. The canon of revelation and the period of legislation are closed. Let no man dare to add to it or take from it, or dilute it, or substitute for it. It is written. It is finished.

II. INDIVIDUALITY

This New Testament law of Christianity segregates the individual from his own family, from society with all its customs and requirements, from race and nationality, from caste, however exclusive, from all governmental control or intimidations, from all the bonds of friendship, though dear as the tie between David and Jonathan or Damon and Pythias, then isolates him from every external influence, strips him of every artificial distinction arising from wealth or poverty or social status, and then shuts him up in an exclusive circle alone with God, who is no respecter of persons, and there demands of his naked and solitary personality a voluntary surrender of his will to God's will and an immediate response of obedience to all its demands. There are no sponsors, or proxies. Enforced or insincere obedience counts nothing at all. The sole responsibility of decision and action rests directly on the individual soul. Each one must give account of himself to God. This is the first principle of New Testament law—to bring each naked soul face to face with God. When that first Baptist voice broke the silence of four hundred years it startled the world with its appeal to individuality "Think not to say within yourselves, we have Abraham to our father. Behold the axe is laid at the root of the trees and every tree that bringeth not forth good fruit is hewn down and cast into the fire." Do thou repent. Do thou confess thy sins. Do thou be baptized. It was the first step of Christianity, and what a colossal stride! Family ties count nothing. Greek culture nothing. Roman citizenship nothing. Circumcision nothing. O soul, thou art alone before God! The multitude shall not swallow thee up. "If thou shalt be wise, thou shalt be wise for thyself; but if thou scornest thou alone shah bear it." Family relationship intruded upon our Lord's busiest hour. "Behold, Thy mother and Thy brothers seek Thee." Once before He had said: "Woman, what have I to do with thee," and now like a flash of lightning comes His scathing reply, "Who is my mother, and who are my brothers? Whosoever doeth the will of my heavenly Father, the same is my mother, my brother, my sister."

Another time it intruded upon Him to call forth His crucial statement: "If any main hate not his father and mother and brother and sister he can not be my disciple."

In His dying hour, on the way to the cross, He heard its voice once more: "Blessed is the womb that bare thee and the paps which gave thee suck," and once more He replied. "Yea, rather blessed is she that doeth the will of God." Superiority for the twelve over Paul was claimed because they had known the Lord in the flesh. But Paul rejoined: "Wherefore henceforth know we no man after the flesh; yea, though we have known Christ after the flesh, yet now henceforth know we him no more."

How often in history has the question been propounded by

some wishing to shun personal responsibility? May I not refer this matter to the magistrates? May I not consult the customs of my country? May I not seek the guidance of my priest and put on him the responsibility of interpreting this book? Nay, verily. Do thou interpret. It is God's letter to thy soul. Thy right of private judgment is the crown jewel of thy humanity. Sometimes even Baptists falter on this point. I have heard one of them excuse himself from an acknowledged duty of co-operation in missions, because his church was opposed to the mission work. Not even thy church can absolve thee from individual duty. Churches are time organizations and are punished in time. They do not stand before the great white throne of judgment. But thy soul shall appear before the Judge. Well did our Lord know that there could be no evangelization of the world if ancestors, families, customs, government, commerce, and priests could stand between the individual soul and God. Thy relation to God is paramount. His law takes precedence of all and swallows up all. In giving emphasis to this doctrine of individuality our Baptist fathers have suffered martyrdom at the hands of the heathen, the Romanist, the Greek, and the Protestant alike.

III. Freedom of Conscience.

This follows from individual responsibility. If one be responsible for himself, there must be no restraint or constraint of his conscience. Neither parent, nor government, nor church, may usurp the prerogative of God as Lord of the conscience. God himself does not coerce the will. His people are volunteers, not conscripts. As has been stated, the prevalent theory in the days of the Reformation was: "Whose is the government—his is the religion." Louis XIV. revoked the Edict of Nantes, signed by his grandfather, the great Henry of Navarre. Calvin burned Servetus at the stake. Luther loosed all the hounds of persecution upon the Baptists, in his day. Holland, the little republic that tore her lowlands from the ocean flood, and for eighty years, by pike and dike, repelled the Spaniard with his inquisition, did herself destroy her greatest statesman, John of Barneveldt, and banish her great historian Grotius for conscience sake. Henry VIII., in England, and his successors, delighted to persecute for conscience' sake. John Knox, of Scotland, so tarnished his great name. The Congregationalists of New England and the Episcopalians of Virginia alike denied freedom of conscience to their fellowmen. There was not a government in the world that allowed full liberty of conscience to all men until a Baptist established the colony of Rhode Island. At a great dining in England John Bright asked a Baptist statesman beside him "What special contribution have your people made to the world?" "Civil and religious liberty," replied the statesman. "A great contribution," replied John Bright. Bancroft, in his history of America, declares: "Freedom of conscience, unlimited freedom of mind, was from the first the trophy of the Baptists." On November 5, 1658, these Baptists thus instructed their agent in England "Plead our case in such sort as we may not be compelled to exercise any civil power over men's consciences; we do judge it no less than a point of absolute cruelty." In their petition to Charles II. They thus urged: "It is much in our hearts to hold forth a lively experiment, that a most flourishing civil state may stand, and best be maintained, with a full liberty of religious concernments." And so when their charter came it provided: *"No person* within the said colony, at any time hereafter, shall be in any wise molested, punished, disquieted, or called in question, for any difference in opinion in matters of religion; *every person* may at all times freely and fully enjoy his own judgment and conscience in matters of religious concernment." And the charter of their great school, now Brown University, has a clause of equal import, a thing unknown at that time in the chartered schools of the whole world.

Freedom of conscience in our day, especially in this country, is a familiar thing. It was not so in earlier days. Pagan, Papist, and Protestant ground liberty of conscience into powder under the iron heel of their despotisms.

IV. SALVATION IS ESSENTIAL TO BAPTISM AND CHURCH MEMBERSHIP.

Here, if nowhere else, Baptists stand absolutely alone. The loot of no other denomination in Christendom rests on this plank. Blood before water—the altar before the lever. This principle eliminates not only all infant baptism and membership, but locates the adult's remission of sins in the fountain of blood instead of the fountain of water. When the author of the letter to the Hebrews declares: "It is not possible that the blood o f bulls and goats should take away sins," he bases the impossibility on the lack of intrinsic merit. Following the precise idea Baptists declare: "It is not possible that the water of baptism should take away sins." There is no intrinsic merit in the water. The blood of Jesus Christ, God's Son, alone can cleanse us from sin. True, the water of baptism and the wine of the Lord's Supper may symbolically take away sins, but not in fact. "Arise and be baptized and wash away thy sins." "This is my blood of the new testament, which is shed for many, for the remission of sins." Both declarations are beautiful and impressive figures of antecedent fact.

A brother of another denomination once objected: "You Baptists have no method of induction into Christ. My people baptize a man into Christ." The reply was two-fold:

(1) It is not enough to get a man into Christ; you must also get Christ into him, as He says, "I in you and you in me." If you insist that baptism really, and not figuratively, puts a man into Christ, how will you meet the Romanist on the other half of it, "Eating the wafer of the Supper really puts Christ into the man. He eats the flesh of the real presence"? You must admit that the words are stronger for his induction than yours.

(2) Baptists have a method of double induction: "We have access *by faith* into this grace wherein we stand." Faith puts us into Christ. "It pleased God to reveal His Son in me." "Christ in you the hope of glory." "Ye are manifestly declared to be an epistle of Christ, * * * written with the Spirit of the

living God * * * in fleshly tables of the heart." "God, who commanded the light to shine out of darkness, hath shined into our hearts, to give the light of the knowledge of the glory of God in the face of Jesus Christ." Thus the Holy Spirit puts Christ in us. We get into Him by faith. He gets into us by the Holy Spirit, thus fulfilling His words: "I in you and you in me."

This great, vital and fundamental Baptist principle, *Salvation must precede ordinances,* does, at one blow, smite and blast those two great enemies of religion, sacramentalism and sacerdotalism. If ritualism saves, priests are a necessity. If my salvation is conditioned on the performance of a rite, then also it is conditioned on the act and will of a third party who administers the saving rite. The doctrine of salvation by rites is the hope of the priest who alone can administer the ripe. This gives both importance and revenue to his office. He multiplies the sacraments. "Two are too few. Let us have seven. The more, the hotter for us, and thus we will control our subjects not only from the cradle to the grave, but from conception in the womb to eternity."

Not only does our great principle destroy both sacramentalism and sacerdotalism, but it alone draws a line of cleavage between the church and the world. To perpetuate the baptism of the unsaved whether infant or adult, tends to blot out from the earth the believer's baptism which Christ appointed. It is a question of discipleship. John the Baptist made disciples before he baptized them. Jesus made disciples before He baptized them (John 4:1). John made disciples by leading them to repentance and faith (Acts 19:4). Jesus made disciples by repentance and faith (Mark 1:15). Jesus commanded: "Go ye therefore and disciple all nations, baptizing them (the discipled)." Draw a perpendicular line. On the right of it write the words, Believers in Christ, Lovers of Christ. On the left of it write the words, Unbelievers in Christ, Haters of Christ. Now, from which side of that line will you take your candidates for baptism? Will you baptize the hating and the unbelieving? You dare not. If from the other side you take them, then already are they God's children, for what saith the scriptures "Whosoever believeth has been born of God. Whosoever loveth is born of God."

Baptists do not bury the living sinner to kill him to sin. But they bury those already dead to sin. For devotion to this principle you may trace our people back by their track of blood, illumined by their fires of martyrdom.

V. THE DOCTRINE OF THE CHURCH.

The church is not the expression of one idea, but of many. Only the most salient and distinctive ideas are here cited

(1) *The church is a spiritual body.*

None but the regenerate should belong to it. It is not a savior, but the home of the saved. I once heard a preacher say: "Join the church if you have no more religion than a horse. Join the church to get religion." When my own soul was concerned about salvation, a preacher urged me to partake of the Lord's Supper in order that I might he converted thereby.

(2) *Separation of Church card State.*

The state, a secular body for secular ends, can never be united to the church, a spiritual body for spiritual ends, without irreparable injury to both. United with the state, the church can never obey Christ: "Be ye not unequally yoked with unbelievers. What part hath he that believeth with an infidel? Come out from among them and be ye separate." There can not be union of church and state without persecution for conscience' sake. There can not be a pure and converted ministry when politicians appoint the preachers. There can not be free speech by the church against national sins when the state holds the purse. See the awful consequences of Luther's mistake on this point in Germany. There, today, the owner of all licensed sins, gambling houses, race tracks, saloons, houses of prostitution, must exhibit certificate of church membership. The blackest pages of American history are those which record the evils of the union of church and state in Massachusetts, Connecticut, and Virginia. And in every one of theme Baptists were persecuted unto blood, stripes, imprisonment and confiscation of property. Massachusetts whipped Obadiah Holmes, imprisoned Clark and banished Roger Williams. At Ashefield, in Connecticut, our Baptist fathers had the choicest parts of their farms and gardens sold under the sheriff's hammer to raise a fund for building a house of worship for another denomination and for the support of its preacher, who had virtually no congregation in that community. In Virginia, Craig, Lunsford, Waller and others were imprisoned. The products of Baptist farms were seized to support a cock-fighting, horseracing, hard-drinking Episcopal ministry. In England and on the continent of Europe time would fail to tell the story of their wrongs, scourgings, cruel mockings, imprisonment and bloody death at the hands of the state church. In every age of the world they have testified for a free church in a free state. From its spiritual nature the church can not rightfully become a political factor. Its members, indeed, as individuals and citizens merely, may align themselves at will with political parties according to each several judgment. On this very account the politician does not court the Baptist church. But any general organization called the church that becomes a mighty political factor, controlling the vote of its members through its clergy, they will court. They censure that church only with bated breath and in confidential whispers. They laud it from the housetops and often make occasion for public eulogiums.

(3) *The church is a particular congregation and not an organized denomination.*

This idea of the church is fundamental and vital and yet least of all understood by the rest of the world—even the religious world. Here, therefore, I would make everything clear and plain. With Greeks, Romanists, Episcopalians, Presbyterians, Methodists, and many others the church is an organized denomination having appellate jurisdiction over its particular congregations. In history, the church as an organized general body, or denomination, has assumed the following forms:

(a) Papistical or autocratic.

It starts with the idea of an earthly head. This autocrat must be the successor of some apostle, himself a primate. Inspiration must rest upon him. All Christendom must be under him. Commencing with the union of church and state under Constantine, the idea reached its final development in the Vatican council, A.D. 1870, which declared the Pope infallible.

(b) Prelatical or episcopal.

That is, the church is a general body, governed by the bishops, bishop now having lost its New Testament meaning.

(c) Presbyterian.

That is, the church is a general body or organized denomination, governed by its presbyters, through synods and general assemblies.

In all of these the particular congregation is under the appellate jurisdiction of the higher power, the General Assembly for the Presbyterians, the General Conference for the Methodists, the Bishops for the Church of England, the Pope for the Romanists. It follows that all these general organizations must have a graded series of courts, ending with a supreme court whose decisions bind all the denomination. And of course these higher courts provide for regular trials, with all necessary forms of law. And also, of course, the sessions of these high courts must last quite a long time in order to attend to all these trials. With all of them the church is an organized denomination having appellate and final jurisdiction over all particular congregations.

Now, in opposition to all these, the Baptists hold that the New Testament church is a particular congregation and not an organized denomination. According to the New Testament: "In Christ, each several building, fitly framed together, groweth into a holy temple in the Lord." Each congregation is a complete temple in itself, and has final jurisdiction over all its affairs. This is the church, to which grievances must be told, and whose decision is final (Matt. 18:15-18). The most forceful and popular objection urged against this idea of the church is that it will be powerless to secure unity of faith, uniformity of discipline, and co-operation in general work among the churches. This objection comes from the view point of human reason. And we frankly admit that whatever theory of the church fails necessarily and generally to secure these great ends discounts itself in probability as scriptural in favor of any other theory which does secure these great ends, simply because we can not conceive of God's wisdom failing. On this account, once in the Northern States of our Union, and more recently in the Southern States, there have been tendencies among Baptists which if they had been successful and followed to their logical consequences would have resulted in this idea of the church:

(d) *A federation,* like the United States.

In this the representative system prevails. Each state selects its representatives, delegates powers to them, projects its sovereignty into the general body, and there merges it into a supreme government for national affairs. These mistaken brethren, North and South, started out with the contention that a Baptist general body, whether district association, state convention, or national convention, *must be composed of churches alone, represented by delegates having delegated powers.* But a Baptist church can not project or merge its sovereignty into a general body of any kind, nor delegate its powers. There is not and cannot be a Baptist federal body. Read again Dr. Wayland's great book, "The Principles and Practices of the Baptists," and there see how the unscriptural idea perished before the wisdom of the brethren. As the good doctor says, "we now wonder that anybody ever supposed that there could be a representative Baptist general body." In like manner, in the South, all attempts to reduce our Southern Baptist Convention or state bodies to this basis have failed for similar good reasons. Our general bodies are purely voluntary, and composed of individuals, not churches. They are solely for counsel and co-operation. They cannot have trials, seeing they possess no ecclesiastical powers. Their sessions have no time for trials, lasting only three or four days. In considering the one question of eligibility for membership in the body they must necessarily act in a summary way on account of time. Their declining to seat any man in no way affects his ecclesiastical status. To ask for regular trial before a Baptist general body, or to claim all the legal forms of procedure in regular courts, whether ecclesiastical or civil, is an absurdity on its face and betrays ignorance of fundamental Baptist principles. It is just upon this point the world, with its graded courts, and other denominations, with their graded courts and regular forms of trial, fail to understand Baptist principles.

They look upon any decision of our general bodies touching membership as similar to the decision of their courts and marvel at our lack of regular forms of trial. The average man thinks of the Methodist Conference and of the Presbyterian Assemblies or of the courts of the country, in deciding upon the merits of a decision on membership by a Baptist general body, and wonders why we do not observe the usual forms of regular courts. They fail to see that a Baptist general body, unlike a Methodist Conference or Presbyterian Assembly, is not and cannot be a court, because with Baptists the church is a particular congregation and not an organized denomination. The particular church is a court and does have its regular forms of trial. No Baptist general body could complete one trial, according to forms of law, in ten years, considering the time at its disposal and the multitude and magnitude of legitimate work that must be considered in its short sessions.

The supreme question then arises, can we with our ideas of the church secure unity of the faith, guard against hurtful schisms, bring about substantial uniformity of discipline, and, above all, secure co-operation in the great departments of work beyond the ability of a single church, namely, missions, education, religious literature, and philanthropy?

It is simply stated as an historical fact, without argument here, that Baptists come nearer to uniformity of faith and discipline and have fewer hurtful schisms than the denominations which seek to secure these results by their iron general organizations. With history before us we are willing to compare results. As to the success of co-operation by our simple methods, we may here in Texas point to a demonstration. Since our session in San Antonio in 187, which eliminated non-cooperation and obstruction, this State Convention has raised more than a million dollars in cash for education, missions, orphanage, church building and other departments of work. We can find no building that will hold our Convention when assembled. Spiritual power, mighty faith, melting prayer, and marvelous unanimity characterize our assemblies. While the world stands this demonstration will avail for justification of our theory of the church.

(4) *The church is a pure democracy.*

Indeed, it is the only one in the world. There is no disbarment of franchise on account of race, education, wealth, age, or sex. In Christ Jesus there is neither Jew nor Greek, barbarian, bond or free, man or woman or child. All its members are equal fellow citizens, and the majority decides. It is of the people, for the people, by the people. This democracy receives and dismisses its members, chooses or deposes its own officers, and manages its own affairs.

(5) *It is the supreme court in Christ's kingdom.*

All cases of discipline come before it, and its decisions are final and irreversible by any human power apart from itself. Of course, it is under law to Christ. It possesses judicial and executive but no legislative powers. Christ is the only law-maker and the New Testament is His law. Its judicial powers cover all cases of grievances and fellowship. It is Christ's court. Our Lord foresaw the inadequacy of secular courts to adjudicate religious differences. The very atmosphere of secular courts is adverse to the religious spirit. Our Lord himself was a victim before the courts of Pilate and Herod. He warned His people that, in every age, they would be dragged before these courts, and clearly foretold what they must expect at the bar of these tribunals. One of the most impressive lessons of the New Testament is the recital of the trials of His ministers before them. Nearly every one of His apostles was put to a violent death by their decisions. Who has not thrilled at the story of Paul before the magistrates at Philippi, before Gallio, Felix, Festus, Agrippa, and Nero? Our Lord carefully provided for *.he settlement of religious differences before His own court. Hear the indignant protest of His apostle against the violators of His law in this respect: "Dare any of you, having a matter against another, go to law before the unjust, and not before the saints? Do ye not know that the saints shall judge the world? And if the world shall be judged by you, are ye unworthy to judge the smallest matters? Know ye not that we shall judge angels? How much more things that pertain to this life! H then ye have judgment of things pertaining to this life, set them to judge who are least esteemed in the church. I speak to your shame. Is it so, that there is not a wise man among you? No, not one that shall be able to judge between his brethren? But brother goeth to law with brother, and that before the unbelievers. Now therefore there is utterly a fault among you, because ye go to law one with another. Why do ye not rather take wrong? Why do ye not rather suffer yourselves to be defrauded?"

(6) The officers of the church are bishops and deacons, the first charged with spiritualities and the second with temporalities.

The idea of a metropolitan bishop, having charge of all the churches of a great city, or of a diocesan bishop, having charge of a province, or state, is of post-apostolic origin and subversive of the scriptural idea of the bishop.

(7) The ordinances of the church are but two, baptism and the Lord's Supper, neither as a means of grace, but both purely figurative and commemorative.

The elements of validity in baptism are (a) it must be by proper authority; (b) its subject is a penitent believer or saved person; (c) the act is immersion; (d) the design is a declaration or confession of faith, symbolizing the cleansing from sin and commemorative of the resurrection. The Supper is a festival observed by the church as a body, and commemorates the atoning death of our Lord and anticipates his second advent. Who may deny that this doctrine of the church is a distinctive principle of the Baptists? Allow me to sum up inn one sentence the complex idea of the church: It is a spiritual body; it must be separated from the state; it is a particular congregation and not an organized denomination, whether Papistical, Episcopal, Presbyterian or federal; it is a pure democracy; it is Christ's executive and judiciary on earth; its officers are bishops and deacons; its ordinances are baptism and the Lord's Supper.

And now, brethren, allow me to put before you a mental diagram embodying the most of what has been said and which itself as a whole is distinctive of the Baptists. We will call it

VI. GOD'S ORDER IN THE GOSPEL OF HIS SON.

Conceive of a circle; in it a man on his knees is reading the New Testament. Both the open book and the man's heart are illumined by the shining of the Holy Spirit. Outside the circle are the man's family, kindred and friends, society and the government. That illumined book is the law of Christianity. The man is individuality, isolated from home, family, kindred, society, and government and shut in with God the Holy Spirit. His conscience is free to decide without embarrassment or hindrance from all external forces or influences. By the Spirit, through the book, his free conscience leads him to an opening in the circle which leads him to salvation. Conviction, changing of his mind, giving of faith on the Spirit's part; the exercise of contrition, repentance, and faith on the man's part. These are the constituent elements of regeneration from both divine and human sides. The man is now justified—saved—a child of God. Here is Christian fellowship. Across the saved man's path runs a river, called baptism. Up through its waters he comes to a door in another circle. This circle is the church, Christ's executive and judiciary. In the center of this circle is the Lord's table. Here is church fellowship and communion. This church is a single congregation, a spiritual body, a pure democracy. Here is the elder or bishop, a simple pastor chosen by the church, and the deacons, who attend to temporal matters. Here is the church conference or court to which brethren bring their grievances for final settlement. Outside in the outlying world are the secular courts.

All along the windings of that river of baptism and its tributaries are other church circles, each complete in itself, each with the Lord's table, and the conference, and the bishop and the deacons. Comity prevails among these churches. There is one law, one Lord, one baptism. A brother in one church, aggrieved against a brother in another church, must carry his case to the church of the offending brother. There is no way to arraign the offending brother before the world's courts without breaking down God's barriers of law and putting religion to open shame.

Out here in territory filled with churches is a convention, state or national. It is a purely co-operative and advisory body. It is composed of individuals, not churches. It is a method, without an iron organization which would swallow up the churches, to elicit, combine and direct the energies and resources of the willing-hearted in all the churches in order to push great movements of evangelization, establish Christian schools, eleemosynary institutions, and devise agencies and means for filling the world with Christian literature, all these mighty enterprises lying beyond the power of a single church.

One successful demonstration that all these great things call be done by a simple and harmless agency of voluntary co-operation of individuals refutes forever the idea of the church as an organized denomination or general body. There is no necessity for it. There is tyranny in it. There is the subversion of Christ's church in it. There is hierarchy in it. My heart exults! My soul leaps for joy that this Convention has furnished proof beyond all successful contradiction that there is no necessity for a hierarchy in order to promote harmony, secure unity of faith and discipline, and to obtain co-operation broad enough and strong enough to do anything God's people ought to do. That demonstration lifts itself up like a granite mountain. Transient clouds of angry criticism hang around its outskirts and splinter their petty lightnings on its adamantine sides. Foul aspersion and misrepresentation may spatter their mud and slime around its base. In the eaves of its foothills a few skulking wolves of prejudice may make their dens and render night hideous by their howlings. But the mountain itself stands immovable and serene. No mists gather about its summit, far above the range and rage of storms. By night the stars silver its crest and by day its halo of sunlight is like the smile of God. This is God's order in the gospel of his Son, and the order is itself a distinctive Baptist principle.

Appendix No. 3

Why Should We Try to Win Protestants to Baptist Views?

WHY SHOULD WE TRY TO WIN PROTESTANTS TO BAPTIST VIEWS?

"But why should we wish to make Baptists of our Protestant brethren? Are not many of them noble Christians—not a few of them among the excellent of the earth? If with their opinions they are so devout and useful, why wish them to adopt other opinions? Yes, there are among them many who command our high admiration for their beautiful Christian character and life; but have a care about your inferences from this fact. The same is true even of many among the Roman Catholics, in the past and in the present; yet who doubts that the Romanist system as a whole is unfavourable to the production of the best types of piety? And it is not necessarily an arrogant and presumptuous thing in us if we strive to bring honored fellow Christians to views which we honestly believe to be more Scriptural, and therefore more wholesome. Apollos was an eloquent man and mighty in the Scriptures, and Aquila and Priscilla were lowly people who doubtless admired him; yet they taught him the way of the Lord 'more perfectly', and no doubt greatly rejoiced that he was willing to learn. He who tries to win people from other denominations to his own distinctive views may be a sectarian bigot; but he may also be a humble and loving Christian."

DR. JOHN A. BROADUS
The Duty of Baptists To Teach Their Distinctive Views (Philadelphia: American Baptist Publication Society, 1881), pages 16-17.

A
Biographical Sketch
of
Benajah Harvey Carroll
(1843-1914)

by
John Franklin Jones

A Biographical Sketch of Benajah Harvey Carroll (1843-1914)

Benajah Harvey Carroll—Civil War soldier (and wounded therein), debater, pastor, professor, editor, denominational leader, author, leading founder of Southwestern Baptist Theological Seminary—was born near Carrolton, Carroll County, Mississippi December 27, 1843. He was one of twelve children born to Benajah and Mary Eliza (Mallard) Carroll. The elder Carroll was a Baptist minister who earned his living by farming. The family moved to Arkansas in 1848 and then to Burleson County, Texas in 1858 (*EoSB*).

The young Carroll entered Baylor University, then located at Independence, Texas, in the fall of 1859 (Lefever, 12). He interrupted his education to enlist in the Texas Ranger Service to guard the Texas frontier in the Civil War. He later enlisted in the regular army in 1862 and was first assigned to the Seventeenth Regiment of Texas Infantry. He served until the end of the Civil War (*EoSB*).

While home on furlough at age eighteen, he married fifteen-year-old Ophelia A Crunk. She refused to return to the Rangers with him and rejected subsequent efforts at the relationship. A brother, with Carroll's consent, sued for divorce on grounds of adultery, and the marriage was dissolved November 9, 1863 (Lefever, 14).

Notwithstanding the interruption of his college education by war, Baylor later granted him the B.A. degree. The University of Tennessee granted him honorary M.A. and D.D. degrees, and Keatchie College, Louisiana, conferred upon him the LL.D. (*EoSB*).

Carroll was converted in 1865 following a bitter struggle with skepticism. He later recounted that skepticism in a sermon, "My Infidelity and What Became of It." He united with the Baptist church at Caldwell in the same year and was ordained to the gospel ministry in the year following (*EoSB*).

Following his years in the war, Carroll preached to small churches in Burleson County, and taught school for three years to pay debts incurred during the war. He served as pastor of the Providence Church, Burleson County and New Hope Church, McLennan County. The First Baptist Church, Waco called him to be its pastor in 1870 and he served that church until 1899, in which year he was elected corresponding secretary for Texas Baptist Education Commission (*EoSB*).

Carroll taught theology and Bible at Baylor from 1872 to 1905. He organized Baylor Theological Seminary in 1904 and played a leading role in founding Southwestern Baptist Theological Seminary. Upon the chartering of that seminary March 14, 1908, Carroll became its president and served in that position until his death. The seminary moved to Ft. Worth in 1990 (*EoSB*).

Carroll was an influential denominational leader. He served on several state and convention committees and made several notable addresses in the interest of several areas of denominational work. He particularly emphasized evangelism, prohibition, Christian education, and home missions (*EoSB*).

He published thirty-three volumes, including special addresses, doctrinal discussions, sermons, and expositions.

BIOGRAPHICAL SKETCH OF B.H. CARROLL

Best known for *An Interpretation of the English Bible*, a commentary of thirteen volumes, his several books of sermons include *Jesus the Christ, Baptists and Their Doctrines, Christ and His Church*. Several volumes of his unpublished materials are extant (*EoSB*).

B. H. Carroll possessed an outstanding personality. He towered several inches over six feet. In his latter years, he wore a flowing white beard. His voice was powerful and pleasing and he was widely known for his oratorical ability and unusual memory (*EoSB*).

Shortly before his death, Carroll summoned Lee R. Scarborough, whom he suggested as his successor at Southwestern (*EoSB*) and said to him:

> If heresy ever comes in the teaching, take it to the faculty. If they will not hear you and take prompt action, take it to the trustees of the Seminary. If they will not hear you, take it to the convention that appoints the Board of Trustees, and if they will no t hear you take it to the great common people of our churches. You will not fail to get a hearing then (Barnes, 205; cited in Lefever, 126, n. 2).

He married Ellen Virginia Bell in 1866. To that union were bon nine children: Hassie, Ellen, Hallie, Jimmy, Gury Sears, B. H. Jr., Charles, Katherine, and Annie Louise. After the death of Ellen, he married Hallie Harison in 1899. To that union with Hallie was born one son, Francis Harrison (*EoSB*). Carroll died at Fort Worth, TX Nov. 11, 1914 (*EoSB*).

SELECTED BIBLIOGRAPHY

Barnes, W. W. *The Southern Baptist Convention, 1845-1953*. Nashville: Broadman, 1954.

Encyclopedia of Southern Baptists. S.v. "Carroll, Benajah Harvey," by Franklin M. Segler, (*EoSB*).

Lefever, Alan J. *Fighting the Good Fight: The Life and Work of Benajah Harvey Carroll.* Austin, TX: Eakin, 1994.

BY JOHN FRANKLIN JONES
CORDOVA, TENNESSEE
MAY 2006

THE BAPTIST STANDARD BEARER, INC.

a non-profit, tax-exempt corporation
committed to the Publication & Preservation
of the Baptist Heritage.

CURRENT TITLES AVAILABLE IN
THE BAPTIST *DISTINCTIVES* SERIES

KIFFIN, WILLIAM   A Sober Discourse of Right to Church-Communion. Wherein is proved by Scripture, the Example of the Primitive Times, and the Practice of All that have Professed the Christian Religion: That no Unbaptized person may be Regularly admitted to the Lord's Supper. (London: George Larkin, 1681).

KINGHORN, JOSEPH   Baptism, A Term of Communion. (Norwich: Bacon, Kinnebrook, and Co., 1816)

KINGHORN, JOSEPH   A Defense of "Baptism, A Term of Communion". In Answer To Robert Hall's Reply. (Norwich: Wilkin and Youngman, 1820).

GILL, JOHN   Gospel Baptism. A Collection of Sermons, Tracts, etc., on Scriptural Authority, the Nature of the New Testament Church and the Ordinance of Baptism by John Gill. (Paris, AR: The Baptist Standard Bearer, Inc., 2006).

CARSON, ALEXANDER	Ecclesiastical Polity of the New Testament. (Dublin: William Carson, 1856).
BOOTH, ABRAHAM	A Defense of the Baptists. A Declaration and Vindication of Three Historically Distinctive Baptist Principles. Compiled and Set Forth in the Republication of Three Books. Revised edition. (Paris, AR: The Baptist Standard Bearer, Inc., 2006).
BOOTH, ABRAHAM	Paedobaptism Examined on the Principles, Concessions, and Reasonings of the Most Learned Paedobaptists. With Replies to the Arguments and Objections of Dr. Williams and Mr. Peter Edwards. 3 volumes. (London: Ebenezer Palmer, 1829).
CARROLL, B. H.	*Ecclesia* - The Church. With an Appendix. (Louisville: Baptist Book Concern, 1903).
CHRISTIAN, JOHN T.	Immersion, The Act of Christian Baptism. (Louisville: Baptist Book Concern, 1891).
FROST, J. M.	Pedobaptism: Is It From Heaven Or Of Men? (Philadelphia: American Baptist Publication Society, 1875).
FULLER, RICHARD	Baptism, and the Terms of Communion; An Argument. (Charleston, SC: Southern Baptist Publication Society, 1854).
GRAVES, J. R.	Tri-Lemma: or, Death By Three Horns. The Presbyterian General Assembly Not Able To Decide This Question: "Is Baptism In The Romish Church Valid?" 1st Edition.

	(Nashville: Southwestern Publishing House, 1861).
MELL, P.H.	Baptism In Its Mode and Subjects. (Charleston, SC: Southern Baptist Publications Society, 1853).
JETER, JEREMIAH B.	Baptist Principles Reset. Consisting of Articles on Distinctive Baptist Principles by Various Authors. With an Appendix. (Richmond: The Religious Herald Co., 1902).
PENDLETON, J.M.	Distinctive Principles of Baptists. (Philadelphia: American Baptist Publication Society, 1882).
THOMAS, JESSE B.	The Church and the Kingdom. A New Testament Study. (Louisville: Baptist Book Concern, 1914).
WALLER, JOHN L.	Open Communion Shown to be Unscriptural & Deleterious. With an introductory essay by Dr. D. R. Campbell and an Appendix. (Louisville: Baptist Book Concern, 1859).

For a complete list of current authors/titles, visit our internet site at:
www.standardbearer.org
or write us at:

he Baptist Standard Bearer, Inc.

NUMBER ONE IRON OAKS DRIVE • PARIS, ARKANSAS 72855
TEL # 479-963-3831   *FAX # 479-963-8083*
EMAIL: Baptist@centurytel.net   http://www.standardbearer.org

Thou hast given a standard to them that fear thee; that it may be displayed because of the truth. — Psalm 60:4

www.ingramcontent.com/pod-product-compliance
Lightning Source LLC
Chambersburg PA
CBHW020803160426
43192CB00006B/416